THE HEALING COMMISSION

WALKING IN DIVINE POWER
AND AUTHORITY

THE HEALING COMMISSION

WALKING IN DIVINE POWER AND AUTHORITY

THOMAS CORNELL

SOZO PUBLISHING

CONTENTS

INTRODUCTION
THE CALL TO HEAL

Healing the sick is not just a ministry for a select few; it is the mandate of every believer. When Jesus walked the earth, He not only preached the Kingdom of God, but He also demonstrated it —by healing the sick, casting out demons, and restoring the broken. He did not separate proclaiming the Kingdom from demonstrating the Kingdom. Wherever the Kingdom of God was preached, healing followed. And then He turned to His disciples and gave them the same commission: "As the Father has sent me, I also send you" (John 20:21). The call to bring the Kingdom of God is a call to heal, restore, and set free.

The question many believers struggle with today is this: Why don't we see more healing? For many, healing is theoretical, a theological concept rather than a present reality. Others have been disappointed—they have prayed, but nothing seemed to happen. Some have been taught wrongly, believing that healing is not always God's will, or that it was only for the apostolic age. Yet, in contrast, Jesus' life and ministry make one thing absolutely clear: Healing is the will of God.

If healing was not God's will, Jesus would have been violating His Father's will every time He healed someone. Yet, in every instance of His ministry, He never turned away a single person who came to Him in faith. He healed all who came (Matthew 12:15). He delivered all who were oppressed (Acts 10:38). And He taught His disciples to do the same: "Preach the Kingdom, heal the sick, cleanse the lepers, cast out demons" (Matthew 10:7-8). This was not a suggestion—it was a command.

The purpose of this book is to demystify healing and make it practical and accessible. Healing is not for the elite. It is not reserved for pastors, prophets, or evangelists. It is for every believer. Jesus never intended for healing to be an occasional miracle—He intended for it to be the natural outflow of the Kingdom.

Healing Is Central to the Kingdom

When Jesus preached, "Repent, for the Kingdom of God is at hand" (Matthew 4:17), He was declaring that His rule had broken into this world. And when His rule enters, sickness, oppression, and darkness must leave. In Revelation 21-22, we see the fullness of God's Kingdom—a reality in which there is no sickness, no pain, no suffering. Why? Because where God rules fully, healing is absolute.

When Jesus healed the sick, He was demonstrating the future reality of the Kingdom in the present. His miracles were not random acts of kindness; they were signs of His dominion, proof that God's rule was invading the earth. Every healing was a collision of two kingdoms—the Kingdom of God overtaking the dominion of darkness.

This is why Jesus did not just say, "I preach the Kingdom"; He said, "If I cast out demons by the Spirit of God, then the

Kingdom of God has come upon you" (Matthew 12:28). Healing, deliverance, and restoration are not side effects of the Gospel; they are the evidence of the Gospel.

Jesus' Mission Is Now Our Mission

In Luke 4:16-21, Jesus stood in the synagogue and read from Isaiah 61:

"The Spirit of the Lord is upon me, because He has anointed me to preach the gospel to the poor; He has sent me to heal the brokenhearted, to proclaim liberty to the captives, and recovery of sight to the blind, to set at liberty those who are oppressed, to proclaim the acceptable year of the Lord."

Then He sat down and boldly declared: "Today this Scripture is fulfilled in your hearing." This was His mission statement—not just to preach the Gospel, but to demonstrate it in power. Jesus was saying, "I have come to bring the Kingdom of God to earth, and this is what it looks like: healing, freedom, and restoration."

But this is not just Jesus' mission—it is ours. In John 20:21, He said, "As the Father has sent Me, I also send you." The same mission He received from the Father, He has now entrusted to us. We are called to bring the Kingdom of God into our world, to demolish the works of the enemy (1 John 3:8), and to see healing, deliverance, and salvation manifest.

The Word "Salvation" Means More Than You Think

Many believers misunderstand the word "salvation." In Matthew 1:21, the angel tells Joseph, "You shall call His name Jesus, for He will save His people from their sins." The Greek word used for "save" is SOZO—which means to save, heal, and deliver.

SOZO is not just about forgiveness of sins—it is about restoring everything that was broken by sin. It means healing the body, soul, and spirit. Jesus did not come just to get people into heaven; He came to bring heaven into people. And part of heaven's reality is divine healing. This is why Psalm 103:2-3 reminds us:

"Bless the Lord, O my soul, and forget not all His benefits—who forgives all your iniquities, who heals all your diseases."

Healing and forgiveness go hand in hand. We should never separate what God has joined together. Jesus paid for our healing at the same time He paid for our sins (Isaiah 53:4-5, 1 Peter 2:24). When He suffered on the cross, He bore both our sins and our sicknesses.

The Commission to Heal the Sick

Healing is not optional for believers—it is a command. In Mark 16:17-18, Jesus said:

"These signs will follow those who believe: In My name they will cast out demons... they will lay hands on the sick, and they will recover."

He did not say, "These signs will follow only the apostles" or "only pastors and evangelists"—He said, "those who believe." If you are a believer, then this mandate applies to you. In Matthew 10:7-8, Jesus gave His disciples a clear instruction:

"As you go, preach, saying, 'The Kingdom of heaven is at hand.' Heal the sick, cleanse the lepers, raise the dead, cast out demons. Freely you have received, freely give."

This is the essence of healing ministry: We have freely received healing through Christ, and now we are to freely give it to others.

Stepping Into Healing Ministry

The purpose of this book is to equip you to pray for the sick with confidence—not as a last resort, but as a first response. You will learn:

- How to operate in faith and see real results
- The biblical foundation for healing and how it is part of the Kingdom
- How to overcome common obstacles to healing
- How to break generational curses and remove hindrances
- How to pray for healing in different settings—church, daily life, evangelism, and missions

Healing ministry is not about formulas—it is about relationship with God. Jesus only did what He saw the Father doing (John 5:19). The more we align with the Father's heart, the more we will see healing flow.

As you read this book, I encourage you to expect—not just to learn about healing, but to experience it. Because the same Jesus who healed then is healing now. And He wants to heal through you.

CHAPTER 1

THE KINGDOM OF GOD
AND THE POWER TO HEAL

When Jesus walked the earth, He carried a message that was far greater than salvation alone—He proclaimed the arrival of the Kingdom of God. His ministry was not just about getting people to heaven; it was about bringing heaven to earth. Every time Jesus healed the sick, cast out demons, or raised the dead, He was demonstrating the reality of His Kingdom. Healing was not an optional side effect of the Gospel—it was proof that God's rule had come near.

The Kingdom of God is the realm where God reigns completely—where there is no sickness, no sin, no oppression, and no death. This is why, in Revelation 21-22, we see a vision of the final and full manifestation of God's Kingdom, where pain and suffering no longer exist. But when Jesus came, He was not just talking about a future Kingdom—He was bringing a present reality.

Jesus' message was simple: "Repent, for the Kingdom of Heaven is at hand" (Matthew 4:17). He was announcing that God's rule had broken into human history. And every time He preached, He healed the sick. The Kingdom of God was not just words—it was power. Jesus Himself explained this connection in Luke 11:20:

"If I cast out demons by the finger of God, then the Kingdom of God has come upon you."

Healing and deliverance were not separate from the Kingdom —they were signs that the Kingdom was present. Wherever the King reigns, the effects of sin and darkness must bow. This is why Jesus told His disciples in Matthew 10:7-8:

"As you go, preach, saying, 'The Kingdom of Heaven is at hand.' Heal the sick, cleanse the lepers, raise the dead, cast out demons. Freely you have received, freely give."

Notice that preaching the Kingdom and healing the sick are linked together. Jesus did not tell His disciples to only preach; He commanded them to demonstrate the message with power.

One of the most profound moments in Jesus' ministry was in Luke 4:16-21, when He stood up in the synagogue and read from Isaiah 61:

"The Spirit of the Lord is upon me, because He has anointed me to preach the gospel to the poor; He has sent me to heal the brokenhearted, to proclaim liberty to the captives, and recovery of sight to the blind, to set at liberty those who are oppressed, to proclaim the acceptable year of the Lord."

Then He sat down and said, "Today, this Scripture is fulfilled in your hearing." Jesus was declaring His mission: to bring the Kingdom of God to earth and to restore what had been broken by sin. Healing the sick was not secondary—it was central to His purpose. And then He did something remarkable. In John 20:21, He turned to His followers and said:

"As the Father has sent Me, I also send you."

Just as Jesus was sent to bring healing and freedom, we are sent to do the same.

Many believers do not realize that healing is not just something we do—it is part of our Kingdom mandate. We are not just called to preach about the Kingdom; we are called to demonstrate the Kingdom through healing, deliverance, and restoration. This is why Mark 16:17-18 says:

> *"These signs will follow those who believe: In My name, they will cast out demons... they will lay hands on the sick, and they will recover."*

Healing is supposed to be the normal lifestyle of a believer, not an occasional event.

Unfortunately, many Christians have separated healing from the Gospel. They see salvation as spiritual and healing as optional. But in Matthew 1:21, the angel told Joseph that Jesus would "save His people from their sins."

The word "save" in Greek is SOZO, which means to save, heal, and deliver. Jesus' mission was not just to forgive sins—it was to heal, restore, and set people free. This is why Psalm 103:2-3 tells us:

> *"Bless the Lord, O my soul, and forget not all His benefits—who forgives all your iniquities, who heals all your diseases."*

Forgiveness and healing go hand in hand. The cross of Christ did not just pay for our sins—it paid for our sicknesses as well. Isaiah 53:4-5 tells us:

"Surely He has borne our griefs and carried our sorrows... by His stripes, we are healed."

And 1 Peter 2:24 confirms:

"By whose stripes, you were healed."

Healing is not something we have to convince God to do—it is something He already paid for in full. When Jesus sent out His disciples, He told them:

"Heal the sick there, and say to them, 'The Kingdom of God has come near to you.'" (Luke 10:9)

Again, healing and the Kingdom go hand in hand. This means that every time we pray for the sick, we are not just asking for a miracle—we are bringing the Kingdom into that situation. Healing is an invasion of heaven into earth. It is a foretaste of the future Kingdom breaking into the present.

If we truly believe that we are ambassadors of the Kingdom, then healing must be part of our daily lives. Jesus never refused to heal anyone who came to Him in faith. He never said healing was not God's will. He healed all who came to Him (Matthew 12:15). And He has not changed. Hebrews 13:8 declares:

"Jesus Christ is the same yesterday, today, and forever."

This means that what He did then, He still does now—and He wants to do it through us. Healing is not just about feeling better—it is about demonstrating the authority of the Kingdom.

Sickness, disease, and oppression are not part of God's Kingdom. When we pray for healing, we are removing what does not belong in His Kingdom. The more we understand the Kingdom, the more we will expect healing to be a normal part of our lives.

As we move forward in this book, we will explore how to walk in this authority, how to pray effectively, and how to release the power of God into every situation. Because the Kingdom of God is not just a message—it is a demonstration of power.

CHAPTER 2

GOD'S WILL TO HEAL

One of the greatest obstacles people face when praying for the sick is the question: "Is it always God's will to heal?" Many believers have been taught that God only heals sometimes, or that healing is a rare sovereign act rather than a part of His consistent nature. Others struggle with doubt because they prayed for healing and didn't see immediate results. These uncertainties can cause people to hesitate when stepping out in faith to pray for others. But Jesus made it clear—healing is not an afterthought; it is central to God's will and His Kingdom.

Throughout Scripture, God is revealed as Jehovah Rapha, "the Lord who heals" (Exodus 15:26). Healing is not just something God does—it is part of who He is. Just as God's nature is love, His nature is also healing and restoration. This means that, just as we would never question whether it is God's will to forgive, we should never question whether it is His will to heal.

When Jesus walked the earth, He never refused to heal anyone who came to Him in faith. Not once did He say, "It is not My Father's will to heal you." Instead, He healed all who came to Him (Matthew 12:15). His life perfectly revealed the will of the

Father (John 14:9), and His actions showed that healing was always part of God's heart for humanity.

In Matthew 8:2-3, a leper approached Jesus and said, "Lord, if You are willing, You can make me clean." This man had faith in Jesus' ability to heal, but he wasn't sure of His willingness. Jesus responded immediately:

"I am willing. Be cleansed."

With those words, Jesus settled the question forever: God is always willing to heal.

Some people argue that sickness is sometimes God's way of teaching us a lesson, or that it is sent by Him to develop our character. But nowhere in the ministry of Jesus do we see Him placing sickness on someone to teach them a lesson. Instead, He treated sickness as an enemy to be destroyed. Acts 10:38 says:

"God anointed Jesus of Nazareth with the Holy Spirit and power, and He went about doing good and healing all who were oppressed by the devil, for God was with Him."

This verse reveals two key truths:

1. Healing is "doing good." It is always an act of God's goodness and mercy.
2. Sickness is called "oppression of the devil." It is not something God gives—it is something He removes.

If sickness were part of God's plan, Jesus would have worked against the Father every time He healed someone. But Jesus said, "I only do what I see My Father doing" (John 5:19). Every healing was a manifestation of God's will. Another powerful proof of God's desire to heal is found in Psalm 103:2-3:

"Bless the Lord, O my soul, and forget not all His benefits—who forgives all your iniquities, who heals all your diseases."

This passage links forgiveness and healing together. Just as salvation is a promise for all, healing is included in God's benefits. If we believe it is always God's will to forgive, we should believe it is always His will to heal. Isaiah 53:4-5 prophesies about Jesus' atoning work:

"Surely He has borne our griefs and carried our sorrows... by His stripes, we are healed."

Some claim that this verse only refers to spiritual healing, but Matthew 8:16-17 directly quotes Isaiah 53 in the context of Jesus physically healing people. The New Testament confirms that Jesus' sacrifice provided for both forgiveness of sin and healing of disease.

When Jesus healed the paralyzed man in Mark 2:1-12, He first said, "Your sins are forgiven." The religious leaders were outraged, thinking He had no authority to forgive sin. Jesus then responded,

"Which is easier: to say to the paralytic, 'Your sins are forgiven,' or to say, 'Get up, take your mat, and walk'? But so that you may know that the Son of Man has authority on earth to forgive sins—He said to the paralytic—'I tell you, get up, take your mat, and go home.'"

Jesus demonstrated that healing and forgiveness go hand in hand. They were both accomplished through His authority, and both are accessible to those who believe.

Some argue that God uses sickness for His glory, citing John 9:1-3, where Jesus healed a man born blind. When asked why the man was born blind, Jesus responded:

"Neither this man nor his parents sinned, but that the works of God should be revealed in him."

Some interpret this as meaning that God caused the blindness so that He could later heal him. But a closer reading of the text reveals that Jesus was not assigning blame or saying that God caused the blindness. Instead, He was shifting the focus to God's desire to heal. The emphasis is on the miracle—not the condition. Jesus immediately healed the man, showing that God's will was for healing, not suffering.

Another common objection is based on Paul's "thorn in the flesh" (2 Corinthians 12:7-10). Some suggest that this was a physical illness that God refused to heal. However, nowhere in the passage does Paul describe his "thorn" as a sickness. Instead, he calls it a messenger of Satan sent to harass him. Throughout the Bible, the term "thorn in the flesh" is used figuratively to describe persecution and opposition, not disease (see Numbers 33:55, Judges 2:3).

Paul was asking for relief from demonic harassment, not physical illness. God's response—"My grace is sufficient for you"—did not mean that healing was denied. It meant that God's power was greater than the opposition Paul faced.

One of the clearest evidences of God's will to heal is the ministry of Jesus' disciples. In Matthew 10:7-8, Jesus commanded them:

"As you go, preach, saying, 'The Kingdom of Heaven is at hand.' Heal the sick, cleanse the lepers, raise the dead, cast out demons. Freely you have received, freely give."

Later, in Acts 3, Peter and John healed a crippled man at the temple gate. They did not pray, "If it is God's will, heal him." Instead, Peter commanded healing:

"In the name of Jesus Christ of Nazareth, rise up and walk!"

This miracle ignited a movement of healing that continued throughout the early church. The disciples did not treat healing as an occasional sovereign act—they treated it as an essential part of their mission.

If healing was only for the apostolic age, why did Jesus say in Mark 16:17-18 that healing would be a sign for all who believe? Why did James instruct the church in James 5:14-15:

"Is anyone among you sick? Let him call for the elders of the church, and let them pray over him, anointing him with oil in the name of the Lord. And the prayer of faith will save the sick, and the Lord will raise him up."

These commands were given to the entire church, not just a select group of apostles. The ministry of healing was never meant to fade away—it is a continuing work of the Kingdom.

Healing is God's will because healing reveals His nature. He is a good Father who delights in making His children whole. Jesus never said, "Wait until heaven to be healed." He healed immediately and told His disciples to do the same.

When we pray for healing, we are not trying to convince God —we are partnering with what He already desires to do. As we step into this truth, we will see greater manifestations of His power, because healing is not just possible—it is promised in the Kingdom of God.

CHAPTER 3

THE AUTHORITY OF THE BELIEVER

ONE OF THE MOST SIGNIFICANT REVELATIONS A believer can receive is the understanding of their authority in Christ. Many Christians pray for healing as if they are asking for a favor, rather than exercising the authority they have been given. When Jesus commanded His disciples to heal the sick, cast out demons, and raise the dead, He did not tell them to ask God to do it—He told them to do it themselves in His name. The difference between asking for healing and declaring healing with authority is often the difference between seeing results or not.

Jesus' ministry was marked by unshakable authority. He did not beg the Father to heal; He spoke with power, and sickness obeyed. In Luke 4:36, the people marveled, saying:

"With authority and power He commands the unclean spirits, and they come out!"

The word "authority" (Greek: exousia) means delegated power, like a police officer enforcing the law. The word "power" (Greek: dunamis) refers to the supernatural force of God. Jesus operated in both. He had the legal right (authority) to heal and the spiritual power (dunamis) to enforce it.

Before Jesus ascended to heaven, He transferred this same authority to His followers. In Matthew 28:18-19, He declared:

"All authority has been given to Me in heaven and on earth. Go therefore..."

The word "therefore" is key. Jesus was saying, "Because I have all authority, I am now giving it to you." We are not waiting for more authority—we have already been given all we need.

Authority Comes From Identity

The problem many believers face is that they do not understand their identity in Christ. They still see themselves as powerless, begging God for what He has already provided. The truth is that the moment we are born again, we are placed in a position of spiritual authority. Ephesians 2:6 says:

"And [God] raised us up together, and made us sit together in the heavenly places in Christ Jesus."

This means we are seated with Christ in a place of dominion. We are not trying to defeat the enemy—he has already been defeated. We are enforcing the victory Jesus already won. This is why Luke 10:19 says:

"Behold, I give you the authority to trample on serpents and scorpions, and over all the power of the enemy, and nothing shall by any means hurt you."

Jesus did not say, "Pray and ask Me to remove the enemy." He said, "I give YOU authority to trample on him."

Healing Through Command, Not Begging

One of the greatest mistakes believers make when praying for healing is asking God to do what He has commanded them to do. Nowhere in the New Testament do we see Jesus or His disciples asking the Father to heal someone. Instead, they commanded healing in Jesus' name.

When Peter and John encountered the lame man at the temple gate in Acts 3, Peter did not say, "Lord, if it be Your will, please heal him." Instead, he declared:

"Silver and gold I do not have, but what I do have I give you: In the name of Jesus Christ of Nazareth, rise up and walk!"

Peter knew what he carried. He did not beg—he commanded healing with authority. And immediately, the man was healed.

Many Christians pray, "God, please heal this person," but Jesus never prayed this way. He simply spoke healing and it manifested.

- To the leper: "Be cleansed!" (Matthew 8:3)
- To the blind man: "Receive your sight!" (Luke 18:42)
- To the dead girl: "Little girl, arise!" (Mark 5:41)
- To the storm: "Peace, be still!" (Mark 4:39)

Jesus did not ask—He commanded. And He expects us to do the same.

Understanding the Power of Jesus' Name

The authority we have is not in ourselves—it is in the name of Jesus. The name of Jesus carries the full backing of heaven. Philippians 2:9-10 says:

"God has highly exalted Him and given Him the name which is above every name, that at the name of Jesus every knee should bow."

Every sickness has a name—cancer, arthritis, diabetes, heart disease. And every name must bow to the name of Jesus. Acts 4:10 explains that healing occurs "by the name of Jesus Christ of Nazareth."

This is why Jesus said in John 14:12-14:

"The works that I do, you will do also, and greater works than these you will do, because I go to My Father. Whatever you ask in My name, that I will do."

When we pray for the sick, we are not asking on our own merit—we are using the authority of His name.

Faith Activates Authority

Authority is only effective when we believe in it and act on it. Many Christians have authority but do not use it. A police officer has authority to stop a speeding car, but if he does not step into the road and enforce it, the car will keep going. In the same way, we can know we have authority, but if we do not step out in faith, sickness will continue unchecked. Jesus told His disciples in Matthew 17:20:

"If you have faith as a mustard seed, you will say to this mountain, 'Move from here to there,' and it will move."

Faith is not passive—it speaks and commands. This is why Mark 11:23 tells us:

"Whoever says to this mountain, 'Be removed and cast into the sea,'

and does not doubt in his heart, but believes that those things he says
will come to pass, he will have whatever he says."

Healing ministry is not about trying to convince God—it is about exercising faith in what He has already provided.

The Roman Centurion: A Model of Faith

One of the greatest demonstrations of faith in Scripture is found in Matthew 8:5-10. A Roman centurion came to Jesus, asking for healing for his servant. But instead of asking Jesus to physically come, he said:

"Lord, I am not worthy that You should come under my roof. But
only speak a word, and my servant will be healed."

Jesus marveled at this statement and said:

"I have not found such great faith, not even in Israel!"

The centurion understood authority. He knew that when Jesus spoke, sickness had to obey. He recognized that Jesus did not need to touch his servant—His word alone carried power.

This is the faith we must have when praying for healing. We are not hoping for something to happen; we are enforcing what Jesus has already done.

Walking in Authority Daily

The key to walking in divine authority is to practice it daily. We must shift our mindset from asking God to move to stepping out in boldness and exercising our authority. Every believer has been given the power to:

- Heal the sick (Mark 16:18)
- Cast out demons (Luke 10:19)
- Speak life over situations (Proverbs 18:21)

The more we act on our authority, the more we will see miracles manifest.

Taking Dominion Over Sickness

Healing is not a special gift for a few—it is the inheritance of every believer. The same Jesus who healed then heals now—and He heals through you.

When we pray for healing, we must do so from a place of authority. We are not begging for a breakthrough—we are enforcing the victory that Jesus has already won. As we step out in faith and exercise our authority, we will see the Kingdom of God manifest in power, just as Jesus promised.

CHAPTER 4

THE FIVE-STEP PRAYER MODEL FOR HEALING

HEALING MINISTRY DOES NOT NEED TO BE complicated. Many people hesitate to pray for the sick because they feel unqualified, uncertain, or afraid that nothing will happen. But Jesus never intended healing prayer to be limited to those with special gifting—He commanded every believer to heal the sick (Matthew 10:7-8, Mark 16:17-18).

One of the most practical ways to approach healing ministry is through a structured prayer model that helps believers pray with confidence and discern the Holy Spirit's leading. Healing is not about performing a ritual—it is about partnering with God. Jesus healed in many different ways—sometimes by speaking a word (Luke 7:7-10), other times by laying on hands (Mark 8:23-25), and sometimes even in unconventional ways, like using mud and spit (John 9:6-7). The key is learning to listen to the Holy Spirit and responding in faith.

This Five-Step Prayer Model is a simple, effective way to pray for healing while staying sensitive to the Holy Spirit. The five steps are:

1. Interview: Ask the person what they need prayer for.
2. Diagnosis: Discern what is causing the condition.
3. Prayer Selection: Pray specifically based on what God reveals.
4. Prayer Engagement: Pray with faith and authority.
5. Reassessment & Post-Prayer Guidance: Check for improvement and encourage next steps.

Step 1: The Interview—What Do You Need Prayer For?

The first step in praying for healing is simply asking the person what they need prayer for. Jesus often asked people what they wanted Him to do (Mark 10:51, John 5:6). Even though He already knew, He wanted them to express their faith by making a request. Ask simple, direct questions such as:

- "What do you need prayer for?"
- "How long have you had this condition?"
- "Have doctors given you a diagnosis?"

This interview is not a medical examination, nor is it meant to embarrass the person. It is a way to engage with the individual and identify the need.

Sometimes, people might not just need physical healing—they may also need inner healing or deliverance from oppression. By asking questions, we open the door for the Holy Spirit to reveal deeper areas that need healing.

Step 2: The Diagnosis—What Is Causing This?

After hearing the request, the next step is to discern what may be causing the condition. Not all sickness is purely physical—some illnesses have spiritual, emotional, or even demonic roots. There are several potential causes of sickness:

- Natural Causes: Injury, genetics, or environmental factors.
- Emotional Causes: Unforgiveness, bitterness, or trauma can lead to physical symptoms (Proverbs 17:22).
- Spiritual Causes: In some cases, sickness may be linked to demonic oppression (Luke 13:11-13).
- Generational Curses: Family patterns of illness may be connected to spiritual strongholds (Exodus 20:5, Galatians 3:13).

Ask the Holy Spirit for discernment to reveal if there is something deeper affecting the person. Sometimes, healing may come through breaking unforgiveness (Mark 11:25) or through deliverance from oppression (Luke 4:18).

Step 3: Prayer Selection—How Should You Pray?

Once you have identified the need, the next step is to determine how to pray. There are different types of healing prayer:

- Commanding Prayer: Speaking directly to the sickness or condition (Mark 11:23).
- Petitioning Prayer: Asking God for intervention (James 5:14-15).
- Intercessory Prayer: Standing in the gap for another person (Job 42:10).
- Deliverance Prayer: Casting out a spirit of infirmity (Luke 13:12-13).
- Blessing Prayer: Declaring God's healing and restoration over the person (Numbers 6:24-26).

For example, if a person has a demonic affliction, a simple prayer for healing may not be enough—they may need deliverance first. If someone is suffering from chronic pain linked to trauma, they may need prayer for emotional healing as well as physical healing. This step requires listening to the Holy Spirit. Often, He will reveal how to pray and what to say.

Step 4: Prayer Engagement—Pray with Faith and Authority

This is where you begin to pray for healing with confidence. The Bible teaches that we are to:

- Lay hands on the sick (Mark 16:18).
- Speak healing in Jesus' name (Acts 3:6).
- Command sickness to leave (Luke 9:1-2).

Here are some key things to remember when praying:

1. Pray with authority: Jesus never begged for healing— He commanded it. Speak with boldness, saying things like:

- "In Jesus' name, I command this pain to leave now."
- "I rebuke this sickness and release healing."

2. Pray with expectation: Jesus said, "They will recover" (Mark 16:18). Pray with faith that healing will happen.

3. Be open to the Holy Spirit: Sometimes God may lead you to pray in a specific way—perhaps using scripture, anointing with oil, or speaking prophetically.

4. Listen and adjust: Healing often happens progressively. Pay attention to any impressions or words from God as you pray.

Step 5: Reassessment & Post-Prayer Guidance

After praying, ask the person: "Do you feel any difference?"

This is a critical step that many believers forget. Jesus often asked people to test their healing (Mark 8:23-25, Luke 17:14). Sometimes healing happens instantly, and other times it is progressive.

If the person reports improvement, thank God and keep praying. Often, a partial healing is an invitation to keep pressing in until full healing manifests. If no improvement is seen, consider:

- Praying again (Jesus prayed twice for a blind man in Mark 8:22-25).
- Asking if there is unforgiveness or emotional wounds that need healing.
- Declaring healing over time (some healings take time to manifest).

Encourage the person to stand in faith and continue declaring God's promise of healing over their life.

Common Obstacles to Healing and How to Address Them

There are times when healing does not manifest immediately. Some possible hindrances include:

- Unbelief (Mark 6:5-6) – Encourage faith and share testimonies of healing.
- Unforgiveness (Mark 11:25) – Encourage the person to forgive.
- Demonic Oppression (Luke 13:11-13) – Consider praying for deliverance.
- Lack of Persistence (Luke 18:1-8) – Encourage the person to keep praying.

Healing is not about human ability—it is about trusting God's power and stepping out in faith. Jesus has already paid for our healing, and He has given us the authority to enforce His victory.

As we continue in this book, we will explore more practical applications of healing prayer and how to grow in confidence as we step into this calling.

CHAPTER 5

KEYS TO INSTANT HEALING

HEALING IS PART OF GOD'S COVENANT WITH HIS people, and throughout Scripture, we see that it is His desire to restore health to those who are sick. While some healings happen gradually, the Bible provides many examples of instant healing—where the power of God touches a person immediately, and their body is restored in a moment. The same power that healed the sick in Jesus' time is still available today, and as believers, we are called to walk in this authority.

Jesus never struggled to heal people. He never hesitated or wondered if healing would manifest. Every time He prayed for the sick, there was a demonstration of power, and many were healed immediately. This chapter will explore the keys to instant healing, helping believers understand how to step into a greater flow of God's healing power.

Understanding the Power of Faith

One of the most common factors in instant healing is faith. Faith is the spiritual currency of the Kingdom, and healing is often released in response to faith. In Mark 5:34, Jesus said to the woman who had suffered from bleeding for twelve years:

"Daughter, your faith has made you well. Go in peace, and be healed of your affliction."

This woman was healed instantly the moment she touched Jesus' garment. It was not simply Jesus' power that healed her—it was her faith that accessed that power. Faith is the certainty that God's will is to heal, and that healing is available right now. Hebrews 11:1 defines faith as:

"Now faith is the substance of things hoped for, the evidence of things not seen."

Faith is present-tense. It does not wait for a future healing—it receives healing as a finished work. Many believers struggle to see instant healing because they are hoping for healing instead of believing it is already available.

Speaking with Authority

Jesus did not pray long, emotional prayers when healing the sick. He spoke with authority and commanded sickness to leave.

- To the blind man: "Receive your sight!" (Luke 18:42)
- To the paralyzed man: "Rise, take up your bed, and walk." (John 5:8)
- To the storm: "Peace, be still!" (Mark 4:39)

Jesus understood that His words carried power. Proverbs 18:21 tells us:

"Death and life are in the power of the tongue, and those who love it will eat its fruit."

When we pray for the sick, we must speak life and command healing. Instead of saying, "Lord, if it be Your will, please heal this person," we should declare:

- "In Jesus' name, be healed right now."
- "I command this pain to leave now."
- "Body, be restored in the name of Jesus."

Healing is often delayed when prayers are passive instead of bold declarations of authority.

Removing Doubt and Unbelief

One of the greatest hindrances to instant healing is doubt. In Mark 6:5-6, it is recorded that Jesus could not do many miracles in His hometown because of their unbelief. The power of God was present, but their lack of faith blocked the flow of healing. James 1:6-7 warns:

"Let him ask in faith, with no doubting, for he who doubts is like a wave of the sea driven and tossed by the wind. Let not that man suppose that he will receive anything from the Lord."

Doubt acts like a barrier between us and the miraculous. If we are unsure whether God wants to heal, we will struggle to see healing manifest. But when we are fully convinced of God's willingness and power to heal, faith is activated, and healing flows freely.

Recognizing the Presence of the Holy Spirit

Healing is not just about words—it is about God's presence moving through us. The Holy Spirit is the active power of God that brings healing. Luke 5:17 tells us:

"The power of the Lord was present to heal them."

There are times when the Holy Spirit's healing presence is tangible, and people are healed instantly. Learning to recognize and cooperate with the Holy Spirit is key to seeing instant healings. Some ways to recognize the Holy Spirit's presence during healing prayer include:

- Heat or tingling in your hands or body.
- A sudden strong faith or boldness rising in your spirit.
- A sense of the anointing increasing in the room.
- A word of knowledge revealing specific conditions that God wants to heal.

When the Holy Spirit is moving, healing often happens quickly and effortlessly.

The Power of Impartation and the Laying on of Hands

Jesus often healed through physical touch. In Mark 16:18, He commanded believers:

"They will lay hands on the sick, and they will recover."

There is a transfer of power when believers lay hands on the sick. In Luke 6:19, it says:

"And the whole multitude sought to touch Him, for power went out from Him and healed them all."

The anointing for healing flows through physical touch. When praying for the sick, placing hands on them as an act of faith can release instant healing.

Healing Through Deliverance

Some sicknesses are caused by spiritual oppression rather than natural conditions. In Luke 13:11-13, Jesus encountered a woman who had been bent over for 18 years. Instead of simply healing her, He cast out a spirit of infirmity:

"Woman, you are loosed from your infirmity."

Immediately, she was healed. This shows that some sicknesses are not medical conditions, but spiritual afflictions. Some signs that a sickness may require deliverance rather than just physical healing include:

- Sudden, unexplainable illnesses.
- Recurring sickness that doctors cannot diagnose.
- Sickness that worsens when prayer begins.
- A family history of the same sickness across generations.

When praying for someone, ask the Holy Spirit if there is a spirit of infirmity at work. If so, command it to leave in Jesus' name.

The Role of Boldness and Persistence

Instant healing does not always happen on the first prayer. In Mark 8:22-25, Jesus prayed twice for a blind man before he was fully healed. This shows that persistence is sometimes required. Luke 18:1-8 teaches the parable of the persistent widow, showing that faith does not give up. Even if healing does not happen immediately, we must continue pressing in until we see breakthrough.

Some people hesitate to pray multiple times, fearing that it shows a lack of faith. But persistence in prayer is not unbelief—it is determination. If Jesus prayed twice for healing, we should not be afraid to do the same.

Walking in Instant Healing

The power to heal is already inside every believer through the Holy Spirit. Instant healing is not a rare event—it is the natural overflow of a life walking in faith, authority, and the presence of God. To see instant healings more frequently:

- Grow in faith by meditating on God's Word.
- Speak healing with boldness and authority.
- Remove doubt and unbelief from your heart.
- Recognize the Holy Spirit's presence and cooperate with Him.
- Lay hands on the sick as an act of faith.
- Be willing to pray multiple times if needed.

Healing is part of the Kingdom mandate given to every believer. As we grow in faith and authority, we will see more and more instant healings, just as Jesus promised in Mark 16:17-18.

CHAPTER 6

THE CONNECTION BETWEEN HEALING, DELIVERANCE, AND BREAKING CURSES

HEALING IS NOT JUST ABOUT PHYSICAL RESTORATION; it is about complete freedom—body, soul, and spirit. Many believers approach healing only from a physical perspective, but the Bible teaches that sickness and disease can also have spiritual roots. Some illnesses are linked to demonic oppression, generational curses, or inner wounds that need healing.

Jesus' ministry was not limited to curing diseases—He also cast out demons and broke spiritual bondages that caused sickness. This means that healing is often connected to deliverance and breaking generational curses. When we address the spiritual roots of sickness, we will see greater and more lasting results in healing prayer.

This chapter will explore the relationship between healing, deliverance, and breaking curses, and how we can effectively minister complete healing to those in need.

Jesus' Ministry: Healing and Deliverance Were Interconnected

Throughout Scripture, we see that healing and deliverance often went hand in hand. Jesus did not treat sickness and demonic oppression as separate issues—He recognized that, in many cases, they were connected. In Luke 13:11-13, Jesus encountered a woman who had been bent over for eighteen years. The Bible says:

> *"And behold, there was a woman who had a spirit of infirmity eighteen years, and was bent over and could in no way raise herself up. But when Jesus saw her, He called her to Him and said to her, 'Woman, you are loosed from your infirmity.' And He laid His hands on her, and immediately she was made straight, and glorified God."*

Notice that Jesus did not just heal her—He loosed her from a spirit of infirmity. This means her sickness was not merely a physical condition—it was demonic in nature. Once the spirit was cast out, her body was healed immediately. In Matthew 8:16-17, we see another example of healing and deliverance working together:

> *"When evening had come, they brought to Him many who were demon-possessed. And He cast out the spirits with a word, and healed all who were sick, that it might be fulfilled which was spoken by Isaiah the prophet, saying: 'He Himself took our infirmities and bore our sicknesses.'"*

Jesus healed and delivered people in the same moment, revealing that sickness is sometimes the result of demonic oppression. This is why we must discern whether a sickness has a natural cause or a spiritual root.

How Demonic Oppression Can Cause Sickness

Not all sickness is caused by demons, but the Bible clearly shows that some diseases and afflictions are spiritually influenced.

Here are some ways demonic oppression can contribute to sickness:

- Spirits of Infirmity – Chronic, long-term illnesses that do not respond to medical treatment.
- Recurring Sickness – Diseases that return even after healing or treatment.
- Unexplainable Pain – Medical professionals cannot find the root cause of the problem.
- Sudden, Severe Illness – A person suddenly becomes sick after an encounter, a traumatic event, or a sinful act.
- Sickness That Gets Worse During Prayer – The person experiences increased pain, anxiety, or resistance when being prayed for.

In cases like these, healing may not manifest fully until the demonic influence is broken. This requires addressing the spiritual strongholds that may be affecting the person's health.

Breaking Generational Curses to Restore Health

Another major source of sickness can be generational curses. Some families experience patterns of disease, mental illness, addiction, or premature death that seem to follow through generations. This is not a coincidence—it is often a spiritual inheritance that must be broken. In Exodus 20:5, God warns that the iniquities of the fathers can affect future generations:

"For I, the Lord your God, am a jealous God, visiting the iniquity of the fathers upon the children to the third and fourth generations of those who hate Me."

This means that sins, covenants, or spiritual influences from our ancestors can bring generational afflictions. However, Jesus became a curse for us to set us free from these inherited bondages. Galatians 3:13 declares:

"Christ has redeemed us from the curse of the law, having become a curse for us."

To break generational curses, believers must:

- Repent of any known sins in their family line.
- Renounce all generational sicknesses, bondages, and afflictions.
- Declare the blood of Jesus over their lives, severing all ungodly ties to the past.

An example prayer to break a generational curse could be:

"In the name of Jesus, I break every generational curse of sickness, disease, and infirmity that has come through my family line. I renounce all agreements with the enemy, and I declare that I am free by the blood of Jesus Christ. Every assignment of sickness against me is canceled, and I receive the healing and wholeness that Jesus paid for at the cross. Amen."

The Role of Forgiveness in Healing and Deliverance

Unforgiveness is one of the biggest open doors for sickness, demonic oppression, and generational curses. Jesus made it clear that if we do not forgive others, we will not be forgiven (Matthew 6:14-15). This includes forgiving family members who may have contributed to generational issues.

Many people who struggle with sickness also struggle with deep wounds from their past. Holding onto bitterness can create spiritual bondage, allowing sickness to take root in the body. When praying for healing, always ask the person if they have any unforgiveness they need to release. As they forgive, healing often flows more freely.

How to Minister Healing, Deliverance, and Freedom

When praying for someone who may be experiencing sickness due to spiritual oppression or a generational curse, follow these steps:

1. Ask Questions and Listen to the Holy Spirit

- Is this a physical condition, a spiritual attack, or both?
- Are there any patterns of sickness in their family?
- Have they experienced trauma, fear, or occult involvement?

2. Lead Them in Repentance and Renunciation

- Guide them in repenting for any personal sins or sins in their family line.
- Have them renounce any demonic agreements, witchcraft, or generational curses.

3. Pray with Authority

- Command spirits of infirmity to leave in Jesus' name.
- Break the power of generational sickness over their body.
- Declare healing and restoration through the power of the Holy Spirit.

4. Lay Hands and Release Healing

- If possible, lay hands on the person as an act of impartation (Mark 16:18).

- Speak specific healing over their body (e.g., "I command this back pain to leave in Jesus' name!").

5. Encourage Faith and Follow-Up

- Have them declare healing scriptures over their life daily.
- Encourage them to walk in their healing and stay connected to strong believers.

Walking in Freedom and Healing

Healing is more than just a physical process—it is a spiritual restoration that often involves deliverance and breaking generational curses. Jesus did not just heal bodies; He set people completely free.

As believers, we are called to minister total healing—body, soul, and spirit. This means addressing the spiritual roots of sickness, standing on the authority of Christ, and breaking every chain that holds people in bondage.

By applying these principles, we will see more effective healings, deeper deliverances, and lasting freedom for those we pray for. The same Jesus who healed then is still healing now—and He is calling His people to set captives free in His name.

CHAPTER 7

BREAKING GENERATIONAL CURSES FOR LASTING HEALING

HEALING IS NOT JUST ABOUT PHYSICAL RESTORATION— it is about complete freedom in Christ. While many sicknesses and diseases have natural causes, some are rooted in spiritual issues, including generational curses. These curses can be the cause of chronic illnesses, repetitive patterns of disease, mental affliction, and even early death in families.

Jesus did not just come to heal sickness; He came to destroy the works of the devil (1 John 3:8). One of the major works of the enemy is keeping people in bondage to generational afflictions. However, through the blood of Jesus, every believer has the power to break free from these inherited curses and walk in lasting healing.

In this chapter, we will explore what generational curses are, how they affect health, and how to break them through the power of Jesus Christ.

What Are Generational Curses?

A generational curse is a spiritual inheritance of affliction that is passed down through family lines. These curses can manifest as:

- Chronic or inherited diseases (e.g., diabetes, heart disease, cancer, mental illness).
- Patterns of premature death (e.g., strokes, suicides, accidents).
- Addictions (e.g., alcoholism, drug abuse, sexual immorality).
- Emotional and mental disorders (e.g., depression, anxiety, bipolar disorder).
- Poverty and financial struggles that seem impossible to break.

The Bible teaches that the sins of the fathers can affect future generations. Exodus 20:5 says:

"For I, the Lord your God, am a jealous God, visiting the iniquity of the fathers upon the children to the third and fourth generations of those who hate Me."

This means that the decisions of past generations can impact their descendants, creating patterns of sickness and oppression. However, God does not leave us without a solution—He provides a way to break free from every curse through the finished work of Jesus Christ.

How Generational Curses Affect Healing

Many people suffer from chronic illnesses and unexplained conditions that do not respond to medical treatment. In some cases, the root cause is not physical but spiritual. If a family has a pattern of sickness or premature death, it may be the result of a generational curse that needs to be broken. Some key signs that a sickness might be linked to a generational curse include:

- The same illness appearing in multiple generations.
- Sudden or early deaths in a family line.
- A recurring affliction that resists medical treatment.
- A sickness that worsens when spiritual warfare increases.

Jesus made it clear that some sicknesses are not just physical ailments but spiritual bondages. In Luke 13:11-13, He healed a woman who had been bent over for eighteen years. Rather than just healing her, He said:

"Woman, you are loosed from your infirmity."

Jesus recognized that her condition was not just medical—it was spiritual. When the spirit of infirmity was cast out, she was instantly healed. This shows us that lasting healing sometimes requires breaking spiritual chains. When we break generational curses, we remove the legal rights that the enemy has to afflict us with disease.

The Biblical Answer to Generational Curses

Many people live in fear of generational curses, believing they are doomed to suffer the same fate as their ancestors. However, the Bible provides a clear path to freedom. Galatians 3:13 declares:

"Christ has redeemed us from the curse of the law, having become a curse for us."

This means that Jesus already broke the power of every curse when He died on the cross. However, for that freedom to manifest in our lives, we must apply His victory through repentance, renunciation, and declaration. 2 Corinthians 5:17 tells us:

"Therefore, if anyone is in Christ, he is a new creation; old things have passed away; behold, all things have become new."

When we are born again, we become part of a new bloodline —the family of Christ. However, many believers still live under the influence of old generational patterns because they have not actively broken ties with them.

How to Break Generational Curses

Breaking a generational curse requires spiritual warfare and faith in the finished work of Christ. Here are the steps to break free and receive lasting healing:

Step 1: Recognize and Identify the Curse

The first step is to ask the Holy Spirit for revelation. Some questions to consider:

- Are there patterns of sickness in your family?
- Has there been a history of premature deaths or recurring diseases?
- Is there evidence of past involvement in witchcraft, idolatry, or false religions?

Ask the Lord to reveal any areas where a curse may be at work in your family line.

Step 2: Repent and Renounce the Curse

Repentance is a powerful key to breaking generational chains. Even though you may not have personally committed the sins of your ancestors, repentance severs any legal access the enemy may have over your life.

Example prayer:

"Father, I repent on behalf of my ancestors for any sins that opened the door to sickness, disease, or oppression in my family line. I renounce all agreements with the enemy, and I reject every generational curse that has been passed down to me. In the name of Jesus, I break all ties to these curses and declare my freedom in Christ. Amen."

Step 3: Declare Your Freedom in Christ

Faith-filled declarations are essential in breaking spiritual bondages. The Bible teaches that our words have power (Proverbs 18:21). Declare these truths over your life:

- "I am redeemed from every curse through the blood of Jesus." (Galatians 3:13)
- "I belong to a new family—the family of God." (2 Corinthians 5:17)
- "No weapon formed against me shall prosper." (Isaiah 54:17)

Speak these truths daily until they become your new reality.

Step 4: Command the Curse to Be Broken

Jesus gave every believer authority to trample over the enemy (Luke 10:19). Using the name of Jesus, command the generational curse to leave your life:

"In the name of Jesus, I break every generational curse of sickness, disease, and infirmity that has been operating in my family. I command all spirits of infirmity and affliction to leave me now. I declare that I am covered by the blood of Jesus and that I walk in divine health. Amen."

Step 5: Walk in Freedom and Healing

After breaking a generational curse, it is important to walk in your newfound freedom. This means:

- Rejecting fear and doubt—the enemy may try to make you think nothing has changed.
- Standing on God's promises—declare healing scriptures daily.
- Living a life of faith and obedience—stay connected to God's Word and fellowship.

Remember, Satan will try to reclaim lost ground, but when you stand firm in your authority, he has no power over you.

Living in the Fullness of Healing and Freedom

Generational curses may have affected your past, but they do not define your future. Jesus has already broken every curse, and He offers complete healing and restoration. The key is applying His victory through repentance, faith, and spiritual warfare.

Healing is not just about removing symptoms—it is about establishing God's Kingdom in every area of your life. As you walk in the truth of God's Word and apply these principles, you will see greater freedom, healing, and victory manifest in your life and the lives of those around you.

CHAPTER 8

HEALING & DELIVERANCE PRAYERS FOR SPECIFIC NEEDS

HEALING AND DELIVERANCE ARE DEEPLY CONNECTED IN Scripture. Jesus did not just heal the sick—He also cast out demons and set captives free from spiritual oppression. Some sicknesses are physical in nature, while others have spiritual roots that require deliverance for complete healing to manifest. Understanding how to pray for specific conditions allows us to minister more effectively and bring lasting freedom to those in need.

In this chapter, we will explore how to pray for healing and deliverance in different situations. We will provide specific prayers and declarations for various conditions, along with biblical foundations to stand on.

Praying for Physical Healing

Many people suffer from chronic illnesses, injuries, or unexplained pain. While some conditions have natural causes, others are linked to spiritual oppression, generational curses, or emotional wounds. Regardless of the cause, God's desire is to heal completely.

General Prayer for Physical Healing

"Heavenly Father, I thank You that You are my healer. Your Word declares that by the stripes of Jesus, I am healed (Isaiah 53:5). Right now, I command all sickness, pain, and disease to leave my body in the name of Jesus. I rebuke every spirit of infirmity and release the healing power of the Holy Spirit over my body. I declare full restoration in Jesus' name. Amen."

Prayer for Chronic Pain

"In the name of Jesus, I command all chronic pain to leave my body. I speak healing to every nerve, muscle, and joint. Pain, I rebuke you, and I command you to go now! Every assignment of the enemy against my health is broken by the blood of Jesus. I receive complete restoration and strength in Jesus' name. Amen."

Prayer for Cancer and Terminal Illness

"Father, You are the God of miracles, and nothing is impossible for You. I renounce every diagnosis of cancer and disease, and I declare healing over my body. I curse every cancerous cell and command it to die in Jesus' name. I speak life and healing to every organ and system in my body. Every spirit of death and destruction is broken off my life. I stand on Your promise that I will live and not die and declare the works of the Lord (Psalm 118:17). In Jesus' name, I receive my healing. Amen."

Praying for Emotional and Inner Healing

Many physical illnesses are linked to emotional wounds, trauma, and unforgiveness. Proverbs 17:22 says, "A cheerful heart is good medicine, but a crushed spirit dries up the bones." Healing is not just about the body—it is about the soul and spirit as well.

Prayer for Emotional Wounds and Trauma

"Father, I bring my heart before You. I give You every pain, every hurt, and every wound from my past. I release every painful memory into Your hands. I ask You to heal my heart and restore my joy. I choose to forgive those who have hurt me, and I declare that I am free from the pain of the past. Fill me with Your peace, Lord. In Jesus' name, Amen."

Prayer for Anxiety and Depression

"In the name of Jesus, I rebuke the spirit of heaviness, anxiety, and fear. I take authority over every lie of the enemy that brings hopelessness. I declare that I have the mind of Christ (1 Corinthians 2:16). I receive the joy of the Lord as my strength. I speak peace over my emotions and declare that I am free from every stronghold of fear. In Jesus' name, Amen."

Prayer for Breaking the Spirit of Suicide

"Father, in Jesus' name, I come against every spirit of death and self-harm. I declare that I am fearfully and wonderfully made (Psalm 139:14). I reject every thought of hopelessness and despair. I break every agreement with the enemy and receive the love and peace of God. I declare that my life has purpose, and I will fulfill the calling God has placed on me. In Jesus' name, Amen."

Praying for Deliverance from Spiritual Oppression

Some sicknesses and conditions have a spiritual root and require deliverance rather than just physical healing. Jesus often cast out spirits of infirmity, showing that sickness can be caused by demonic oppression (Luke 13:11-13).

Prayer for Deliverance from a Spirit of Infirmity

"In the name of Jesus, I take authority over every spirit of infirmity attacking my body. I command every unclean spirit bringing pain, weakness, and disease to leave me now. I declare that my body is a temple of the Holy Spirit, and no demonic power has authority over me. By the blood of Jesus, I am set free. Amen."

Prayer for Breaking Generational Curses of Sickness

"Father, I break every generational curse of sickness, disease, and infirmity in my family line. I renounce every covenant, word, and agreement that has brought sickness into my bloodline. In the name of Jesus, I declare that I am covered by the blood of Christ and that all generational afflictions are broken. I walk in divine health and freedom. Amen."

Prayer for Freedom from Witchcraft and Occult Bondage

"In the mighty name of Jesus, I break every curse, spell, and demonic assignment sent against my life. I renounce all agreements with the kingdom of darkness. I cancel every word spoken over me that is not from God. I cover myself with the blood of Jesus and declare that no weapon formed against me shall prosper (Isaiah 54:17). I walk in the power and authority of Christ. Amen."

Praying for Healing in Relationships and Family

Unforgiveness and broken relationships can hinder healing. When we walk in bitterness, we create a spiritual barrier that prevents the flow of God's power.

Prayer for Reconciliation in Relationships

"Father, I bring this broken relationship before You. I ask for Your healing and restoration. Give me the grace to forgive and the

wisdom to rebuild trust. Soften my heart and the heart of the other person. Let Your peace reign in our relationship. In Jesus' name, Amen."

Prayer for Breaking Family Dysfunction and Division

"In the name of Jesus, I break every stronghold of division, strife, and misunderstanding in my family. I declare that my household is under the authority of Jesus Christ. Every plan of the enemy to bring conflict is canceled. I speak love, unity, and restoration over my family. In Jesus' name, Amen."

Walking in Healing and Deliverance Daily

Healing and deliverance are not just one-time events—they are a lifestyle. To maintain freedom, believers must:

- Stay in God's Word – The truth sets us free (John 8:32).
- Guard their minds and hearts – Reject lies and walk in faith.
- Stay in a community of faith – Healing often comes through the Body of Christ.
- Use the authority given by Jesus – Declare healing over their own lives daily.

Healing is not just about removing sickness; it is about walking in divine health and freedom. As we learn to pray with boldness and faith, we will see more consistent breakthroughs and lasting results.

A Call to Minister Healing and Freedom

God has called every believer to walk in healing and deliverance. As we grow in our understanding of how to pray for specific needs, we will see the power of God move more frequently. Jesus gave us authority over sickness and demons, and He calls us to use that authority to bring healing and freedom to the world.

This chapter serves as a guide, but the most important factor in healing and deliverance prayer is listening to the Holy Spirit. When we yield to Him, He will show us exactly how to pray, and we will see His power at work in miraculous ways.

CHAPTER 9

HEALING IN THE CHURCH

HEALING WAS ALWAYS MEANT TO BE A CENTRAL PART OF the church. When Jesus commissioned His disciples, He told them not only to preach the gospel but also to heal the sick, cast out demons, and set captives free (Matthew 10:7-8, Mark 16:17-18). Healing is not a side issue—it is a core function of the body of Christ.

Yet in many churches today, healing is either neglected or seen as something rare and extraordinary. Many believers assume that miracles were for Bible times, but that they are not for today. Others are unsure how to pray for healing and are afraid of what will happen if nothing changes.

However, Scripture shows us that healing was never meant to be occasional or exceptional—it was meant to be normal in the church. The early church operated in healing power daily, and as the church today, we must reclaim this essential part of our calling.

In this chapter, we will explore how to establish a culture of healing in the church, how to train and equip believers to pray for the sick, and how to create an environment where God's healing power flows consistently.

The Early Church and the Ministry of Healing

The book of Acts is filled with examples of the early church moving in healing power. Healing was not reserved for a few apostles—it was part of the normal life of believers.

- Acts 3:6-8 – Peter heals the lame man at the temple gate: "Silver and gold I do not have, but what I do have I give you: In the name of Jesus Christ of Nazareth, rise up and walk."
- Acts 5:12-16 – People brought the sick into the streets, and "they were all healed."
- Acts 9:32-35 – Peter heals Aeneas, and as a result, "all who lived in Lydda and Sharon turned to the Lord."
- Acts 14:8-10 – Paul commands a crippled man to stand, and he is instantly healed.
- Acts 19:11-12 – Paul's handkerchiefs and aprons carry healing power to the sick.
- James 5:14-16 – James commands the elders of the church to pray for the sick and anoint them with oil, declaring that "the prayer of faith will save the sick, and the Lord will raise him up."

Healing was a standard practice in the early church, and it should be standard today. The church was not just a place of teaching and worship—it was a place of miracles, healing, and restoration.

Why Many Churches Do Not See Healing Today

If healing was so normal in the early church, why do many churches today struggle to see it? Here are a few key reasons:

- Lack of Teaching – Many churches do not teach about healing or expect it to happen.
- Fear of Failure – Some leaders avoid healing ministry because they are afraid "what if nothing happens?"
- Theological Uncertainty – Some believe healing ended with the apostles, even though Scripture does not support this view.
- Disconnection from the Holy Spirit – Some churches rely on tradition and programs but do not actively seek the power of the Holy Spirit.

Healing does not happen automatically—it happens when we step out in faith and expect God to move.

How to Build a Culture of Healing in the Church

Creating an atmosphere of healing requires intentionality. The church must actively teach, model, and encourage healing ministry. Here are some ways to develop a healing culture in the local church:

Preach and Teach Healing Regularly

Faith comes by hearing (Romans 10:17). If churches do not teach on healing, people will not have faith for it. Sermons should regularly include:

- Jesus' healings and His commission to believers.
- The promises of healing in Scripture.
- Testimonies of healing to build faith.
- When healing is preached consistently, faith begins to rise, and people expect miracles.

Train and Equip Believers to Pray for the Sick

Healing is not just for pastors and leaders—it is for every believer. The church should train its members on:

- How to lay hands on the sick with faith (Mark 16:18).
- How to listen to the Holy Spirit and receive words of knowledge.
- How to overcome fear and doubt when praying for healing.

Holding healing training sessions and workshops can help believers grow in confidence.

Create Opportunities for Healing Prayer

Churches that see healing consistently make room for it. Some ways to encourage healing prayer include:

- Altar calls for healing during services.
- Special healing nights or miracle services.
- Healing teams available after every service.

Healing will not become normal until people have a regular opportunity to step out in faith and pray for the sick.

Encourage Testimonies of Healing

One of the most powerful ways to build faith for healing is to share testimonies. Revelation 12:11 says:

"They overcame him by the blood of the Lamb and by the word of their testimony."

When someone is healed, they should testify so others can hear and believe. Testimonies create an expectation that God will do it again.

Healing and Deliverance in the Church

Many times, healing ministry in the church must also include deliverance ministry. Some people are not just sick—they are oppressed by spirits of infirmity, fear, or affliction. Jesus regularly cast out demons before healing people. In Luke 13:11-13, He healed a woman who had been crippled by a demonic spirit for eighteen years. When He commanded the spirit to leave, she was immediately healed. Churches should be trained to recognize when sickness is caused by:

- A spirit of infirmity.
- Generational curses affecting a person's health.
- Emotional wounds or trauma that open the door to sickness.

When churches incorporate both healing and deliverance, they see more breakthroughs and lasting results.

The Role of Leadership in Healing Ministry

For healing to become a regular part of church life, leadership must model it first. Leaders must:

- Pray for the sick boldly and expect healing.
- Demonstrate how to listen to the Holy Spirit for healing direction.
- Encourage others to step out in faith and pray for healing.

When pastors and leaders actively participate in healing ministry, it encourages the entire congregation to believe and step out in faith.

Healing as a Tool for Evangelism

Healing is not just for the church—it is also a tool for evangelism. In the book of Acts, miracles led to mass salvations:

- Acts 3:8-10 – The healing of the lame man caused people to believe in Christ.
- Acts 9:34-35 – The healing of Aeneas led an entire town to turn to the Lord.
- Acts 14:8-10 – Paul healed a crippled man, leading to many conversions.

Churches should encourage believers to pray for healing in everyday life—at work, at school, in grocery stores, and on the streets. When people see miracles, they become open to the gospel.

Reclaiming Healing in the Church

Healing was never meant to be rare—it was meant to be normal in the life of the church. To see more healing, churches must:

1. Teach and preach healing consistently.
2. Train and equip believers to pray for the sick.
3. Create opportunities for healing prayer.
4. Encourage testimonies of healing.
5. Recognize when deliverance is needed.
6. Model healing through leadership.
7. Use healing as a tool for evangelism.

As the church embraces healing ministry again, we will see more miracles, more salvations, and more of the power of God released in our communities. Healing is part of our Kingdom mandate—it is time for the church to rise up and walk in its full inheritance.

CHAPTER 10

HEALING IN EVERYDAY LIFE

HEALING WAS NEVER MEANT TO BE LIMITED TO THE four walls of the church. Jesus healed people wherever He went—on the streets, in homes, at wells, in synagogues, and even in grave-yards. His ministry was not confined to religious gatherings; it was a lifestyle of releasing the Kingdom of God.

As believers, we are called to do the same. Healing should not just happen in church services but in everyday life—at work, in schools, in grocery stores, at family gatherings, and wherever people are in need. Many people will never step into a church, but they will encounter believers who carry the power and presence of Jesus.

In this chapter, we will explore how to develop a lifestyle of healing, how to overcome fear when praying for people in public, and how to release God's power in everyday situations.

Healing Was a Lifestyle for Jesus

Jesus modeled what it looks like to live a life where healing was normal and natural. He did not wait for people to come to Him —He met them in their everyday lives.

- In homes – Jesus healed Peter's mother-in-law while visiting Peter's house (Matthew 8:14-15).
- On the streets – He healed blind Bartimaeus while walking through Jericho (Mark 10:46-52).
- At wells – He ministered healing and deliverance to the Samaritan woman at the well (John 4:4-29).
- During meals – He healed a man with dropsy at a Pharisee's house (Luke 14:1-4).
- At funerals – He raised the widow's son from the dead during a funeral procession (Luke 7:11-17).
- In unexpected encounters – He healed a woman who touched His garment in a crowd (Mark 5:25-34).

Healing was woven into the fabric of His daily life, and as His disciples, we are called to follow in His footsteps.

Healing Is Part of the Great Commission

Jesus did not tell His disciples to wait for people to come to them—He commanded them to go and heal the sick. In Matthew 10:7-8, He instructed them:

"As you go, preach, saying, 'The Kingdom of Heaven is at hand.' Heal the sick, cleanse the lepers, raise the dead, cast out demons. Freely you have received, freely give."

The phrase "As you go" means healing should be a part of our daily lives. Whether we are at work, in a store, or at a gas station, we should be ready to pray for those in need.

Overcoming Fear in Public Healing Ministry

Many believers hesitate to pray for healing in public because of fear. Common fears include:

- What if nothing happens?
- What if the person rejects me?
- What will people think of me?

Fear is one of the enemy's biggest weapons to keep believers from stepping out in faith. However, fear is a lie that must be confronted with the truth of God's Word.

Fear of Failure

Many people fear that if they pray and nothing happens, they will look foolish. But healing is God's job, not ours. Our responsibility is to step out in obedience—the results are up to Him.

- Mark 16:17-18 – *"These signs will follow those who believe... they will lay hands on the sick, and they will recover."*
- 1 Corinthians 2:4-5 – *"My speech and my preaching were not with persuasive words of human wisdom, but in demonstration of the Spirit and of power, that your faith should not be in the wisdom of men but in the power of God."*

God does not expect us to perform miracles—He simply calls us to act in faith.

Fear of Rejection

Another common fear is being rejected or feeling awkward if someone says no to prayer. However, rejection is not personal—it is simply a choice people make. Jesus Himself was rejected by many, yet He kept ministering. When offering to pray for someone, be kind and respectful. A simple approach is:

"Hey, I noticed you're in pain. I believe in Jesus, and I've seen Him heal people before. Can I say a quick prayer for you?"

Most people are open to receiving prayer, especially when they are hurting. Even if they say no, you have still planted a seed of God's love.

How to Pray for Healing in Everyday Situations

Healing does not have to be dramatic or complicated. Here are some simple ways to pray for people in everyday life:

Praying for Someone at Work

If a coworker is sick or in pain, offer to pray for them. Many people are open to prayer, especially when they are suffering. You can say:

"I see you're not feeling well. Would it be okay if I prayed for you? It will only take a few seconds."

Keep your prayer brief, simple, and faith-filled.

Example Prayer:

"Father, in the name of Jesus, I command this pain to leave. I speak healing and strength over this body. Thank You, Lord, for restoring health right now. In Jesus' name, Amen."

Praying for Someone in a Store or Public Place

If you see someone limping or wearing a brace, consider offering prayer. A simple way to start is by saying:

"Hey, I couldn't help but notice you're in pain. I've seen Jesus heal people before—would you mind if I prayed for you really quick?"

If they say yes, place your hand (if they are comfortable) on their shoulder or arm and pray with authority.

Praying for Family Members

Healing starts at home. If a family member is sick, do not hesitate to pray for them. Lay hands on them and pray with confidence.

Recognizing Opportunities for Healing Ministry

Healing opportunities are everywhere, but we must learn to recognize them. The Holy Spirit often nudges us when someone needs prayer. Some signs include:

- Noticing someone in pain (limping, wincing, wearing a brace).
- Feeling a strong urge to approach someone.
- Receiving a word of knowledge (an impression, vision, or thought about someone's condition).
- Hearing someone mention their sickness in conversation.

When we pay attention to the Holy Spirit's leading, we will find more opportunities to minister healing.

Healing as a Doorway to Evangelism

Healing often opens people's hearts to Jesus. In the Bible, miracles led to salvation:

- Acts 3:8-10 – The healing of the lame man caused many to believe.
- Acts 8:6-8 – Philip's healing ministry in Samaria led to great joy and conversions.
- Acts 9:32-35 – The healing of Aeneas led an entire town to turn to Jesus.

Healing is a powerful evangelistic tool. Many people are skeptical of Christianity, but when they experience the power of God firsthand, their hearts open to the gospel. When someone is healed, always point them to Jesus:

"This is not about me—Jesus just healed you because He loves you. Do you know Him personally?"

This can lead to deeper conversations about salvation and God's plan for their life.

Making Healing a Daily Habit

To make healing a natural part of life, we must:

- Pray for healing daily – Ask God to show you who to pray for.
- Stay sensitive to the Holy Spirit – He will guide you to those who need healing.
- Step out in faith – The more you pray for the sick, the more you will see results.
- Celebrate testimonies – Thank God for every healing, no matter how small.

Healing is not reserved for church services—it is meant to

happen everywhere we go. As we develop a lifestyle of healing, we will see the Kingdom of God advance in powerful ways.

Becoming a Vessel of Healing in the World

Healing is not just for pastors, evangelists, or special anointed ministers—it is for every believer. Jesus commanded all His disciples to lay hands on the sick and see them recover (Mark 16:18). The world is full of people in pain, waiting for someone to bring them the hope of healing.

As we step out in faith, healing will become a normal part of our everyday lives, just as it was for Jesus and the early church. The Kingdom of God is within us, and as we go, we are called to release it to the world.

CHAPTER 11

THE ROLE OF FAITH IN HEALING

FAITH IS THE FOUNDATION OF HEALING MINISTRY. Throughout Scripture, we see a direct connection between faith and healing. Jesus repeatedly emphasized the importance of faith when healing the sick, and He often told those who were healed, "Your faith has made you well" (Mark 5:34).

Faith is the bridge between God's power and our healing. It is the key that unlocks the miraculous and allows us to step into the supernatural. Yet, many people struggle to understand what faith really is, how it operates, and how to grow in faith to see greater healing.

This chapter will explore the role of faith in healing, common obstacles to faith, and practical ways to develop strong faith that produces results.

Jesus' Teachings on Faith and Healing

Jesus consistently linked faith and healing together. He never made excuses for a lack of healing; instead, He pointed people to faith as the key to receiving.

The Woman with the Issue of Blood

In Mark 5:25-34, a woman who had been bleeding for twelve years touched the hem of Jesus' garment and was instantly healed. Jesus turned to her and said:

"Daughter, your faith has made you well. Go in peace, and be healed of your affliction."

It was not just Jesus' power that healed her—it was her faith that accessed that power.

The Blind Men Who Followed Jesus

In Matthew 9:27-30, two blind men followed Jesus, crying out for mercy. Jesus asked them:

"Do you believe that I am able to do this?"

They replied, "Yes, Lord." Then He said:
"According to your faith, let it be to you."

And immediately, their eyes were opened.

The Centurion's Great Faith

In Matthew 8:5-13, a Roman centurion came to Jesus asking for healing for his servant. Instead of asking Jesus to come to his house, he said:

"Just say the word, and my servant will be healed."

Jesus marveled at his faith, saying:

"I have not found such great faith, not even in Israel!"

And at that moment, his servant was healed. These passages reveal a powerful truth: Faith activates healing. When people approached Jesus with faith, healing was the result.

What Is Faith?

Many people misunderstand faith. Faith is not wishful thinking or hoping something might happen—it is a deep, unshakable confidence in God's will and His power.

Faith Is the Substance of What We Hope For

Hebrews 11:1 gives us a biblical definition of faith:

"Now faith is the substance of things hoped for, the evidence of things not seen."

Faith is not based on what we see—it is based on what God has said. Even if symptoms remain, faith believes that healing is already done because God's Word is true.

Faith Comes from Hearing the Word of God

Romans 10:17 tells us:

"So then faith comes by hearing, and hearing by the word of God."

The more we fill our hearts with God's promises of healing, the stronger our faith becomes. Faith does not grow through emotions—it grows through the Word.

Overcoming Obstacles to Faith

Many believers struggle to see healing because their faith is hindered by doubt, fear, or unbelief. Here are common obstacles to faith and how to overcome them:

Doubt and Unbelief

Doubt is the enemy of faith. In Matthew 13:58, the Bible says that Jesus could not do many miracles in His hometown because of their unbelief. James 1:6-7 warns us:

"But let him ask in faith, with no doubting, for he who doubts is like a wave of the sea driven and tossed by the wind. Let not that man suppose that he will receive anything from the Lord."

How to Overcome Doubt:

- Meditate on healing scriptures daily.
- Surround yourself with testimonies of healing.
- Speak faith-filled declarations over your life.

Fear of Disappointment

Some people fear that if they believe for healing and do not receive it, they will be disappointed. However, fear of disappointment is actually a form of unbelief—it doubts God's faithfulness.

How to Overcome Fear:

- Trust in God's goodness, not just in the outcome.
- Remind yourself that healing is a promise, not a gamble.
- Keep praying even when you don't see immediate results.

Negative Past Experiences

Some people prayed for healing before but did not see results, leading them to believe that healing is not for them. However, past experiences do not change God's truth.

How to Overcome Past Disappointments:

- Refuse to base your theology on experience—base it on the Word.
- Persevere in faith, knowing that delay is not denial.
- •Look at the testimonies of others to build your faith.

How to Grow in Faith for Healing

Faith is like a muscle—it grows as we use it. Here are practical ways to increase your faith for healing:

Meditate on God's Promises Daily

The more you fill your heart with healing scriptures, the more your faith will grow. Some powerful verses to meditate on include:

- Isaiah 53:5 – "By His stripes, we are healed."
- Psalm 103:2-3 – "He forgives all your iniquities, He heals all your diseases."
- Mark 16:17-18 – "They will lay hands on the sick, and they will recover."

Speak Faith-Filled Declarations

Proverbs 18:21 says:

"Death and life are in the power of the tongue."

Instead of speaking sickness, speak life and healing:

- "My body is healed in Jesus' name."
- "I reject sickness and receive divine health."
- "The same Spirit that raised Jesus from the dead gives life to my body." (Romans 8:11)

Step Out and Pray for the Sick

Faith grows through action. The more you pray for others, the more miracles you will see. Jesus told His disciples in Matthew 10:7-8:

"As you go, preach, saying, 'The Kingdom of Heaven is at hand.' Heal the sick, cleanse the lepers, raise the dead, cast out demons."

Healing was not meant to be just for a few special people—it is for every believer. The more you step out, the more your faith will grow.

Faith in Action: Testimonies Build Faith

One of the best ways to strengthen faith is through hearing and sharing testimonies. Revelation 12:11 says:

"They overcame him by the blood of the Lamb and by the word of their testimony."

Every time we share a healing testimony, we:

- Build faith in others.
- Remind ourselves of God's power.
- Create an expectation for more miracles.

If you are believing for healing, surround yourself with stories of God's power. Testimonies remind us that if God did it before, He can do it again.

Living by Faith, Walking in Healing

Faith is the foundation of healing. Without faith, it is impossible to please God (Hebrews 11:6). Healing is not about hoping something might happen—it is about believing in what Jesus already paid for.

As you develop strong faith, you will:

- See more healings in your own life.
- Pray for others with greater confidence.
- Walk in the supernatural power of God.

Faith is not a feeling—it is a decision to believe God's Word over circumstances. As you build your faith daily, you will step into a lifestyle of healing, miracles, and breakthrough.

CHAPTER 12

THE POWER OF PERSISTENT PRAYER IN HEALING

HEALING IS SOMETIMES INSTANT, BUT OTHER TIMES, IT requires persistence. Many people expect healing to happen immediately, and when they do not see instant results, they become discouraged and give up. However, the Bible teaches that perseverance in prayer is often required to see breakthrough.

Persistent prayer does not mean begging God—it means standing in faith until healing manifests. In this chapter, we will explore the biblical foundation for persistence in healing prayer, how to remain steadfast even when results are delayed, and practical ways to keep praying until the breakthrough comes.

Why Persistence in Prayer Is Necessary

Some healings happen immediately, but others take time and persistence. There are many reasons why healing may not manifest right away:

- Spiritual resistance – Daniel prayed for 21 days before his answer came because of spiritual warfare (Daniel 10:12-13).

- Faith development – God sometimes allows a delay so that we grow stronger in faith (James 1:3-4).
- Progressive healing – Some healings unfold over time rather than happening in a single moment (Mark 8:22-25).
- Breaking demonic strongholds – Some illnesses are linked to demonic oppression, requiring persistent warfare (Luke 13:11-13).

Just because healing is not instant does not mean it is not happening.

Jesus Taught Persistence in Prayer

Jesus gave several parables emphasizing the importance of persistence in prayer:

The Persistent Widow (Luke 18:1-8)

Jesus told a parable about a widow who kept demanding justice from an unjust judge. Because of her persistence, the judge finally gave her what she asked for.

Jesus concluded:

"Will not God bring about justice for His chosen ones, who cry out to Him day and night? Will He keep putting them off? I tell you, He will see that they get justice, and quickly." (Luke 18:7-8)

If persistence moves an unjust judge, how much more will it move our loving Father?

The Friend at Midnight (Luke 11:5-10)

Jesus told another parable of a man who persistently knocked on his friend's door at midnight, asking for bread. Because of his boldness and persistence, his request was granted. Jesus then said:

"Ask, and it will be given to you; seek, and you will find; knock, and the door will be opened to you." (Luke 11:9)

The Greek words for "ask," "seek," and "knock" imply continuous action—meaning we must keep asking, keep seeking, and keep knocking. These parables show that persistence in prayer is not a lack of faith—it is proof of faith.

Jesus Himself Prayed More Than Once for Healing

Some people assume that if healing does not happen instantly, they should stop praying. However, even Jesus prayed more than once for healing!

The Blind Man at Bethsaida (Mark 8:22-25)

Jesus prayed for a blind man, and at first, his healing was only partial—he saw "men like trees walking." So Jesus laid hands on him again, and his sight was fully restored. If Jesus prayed twice, then we should not hesitate to keep praying until full healing manifests.

The Ten Lepers (Luke 17:11-14)

Jesus told ten lepers to go show themselves to the priests, and as they went, they were cleansed. This shows that healing can happen progressively. They were not healed instantly, but as they obeyed in faith, healing manifested. This means that if healing does not happen immediately, we should keep praying and believing.

The Power of Agreement in Persistent Prayer

Healing prayer is often strengthened when others join in agreement. Jesus said in Matthew 18:19-20:

"If two of you agree on earth about anything they ask, it will be done for them by my Father in heaven. For where two or three gather in my name, there am I with them."

This is why:

- Having elders lay hands on the sick (James 5:14-15) is important.
- Interceding together as a church brings breakthrough.
- Testimonies help build faith and agreement.

Persistent healing prayer is often a community effort, not just an individual one.

How to Stay Persistent in Healing Prayer

Many people start praying for healing with enthusiasm, but when results are delayed, they lose faith and stop. Here are practical ways to stay persistent:

A. Declare Healing Daily

Faith comes by hearing (Romans 10:17). Instead of focusing on symptoms, declare God's Word:

- "By His stripes, I am healed." (Isaiah 53:5)
- "He heals all my diseases." (Psalm 103:3)
- "No weapon formed against me shall prosper." (Isaiah 54:17)

B. Keep Praying Until the Breakthrough Comes

Jesus said "they will lay hands on the sick, and they will recover" (Mark 16:18). The word "recover" implies a process. If healing does not happen immediately:

- Keep thanking God for His promise.
- Keep resisting sickness and standing in faith.
- Keep speaking life and health over your body.

C. Fast and Pray for Healing Breakthroughs

Some battles require fasting and prayer. In Matthew 17:21, Jesus said:

> *"This kind does not go out except by prayer and fasting."*

Fasting:

- Helps us focus on God's power.
- Breaks spiritual strongholds.
- Increases our sensitivity to the Holy Spirit.

D. Do Not Give Up

Galatians 6:9 encourages us:

> *"Let us not grow weary in doing good, for at the proper time we will reap a harvest if we do not give up."*

Satan wants believers to quit praying, but God's promise remains true—if we persist, we will see results.

Testimonies of Persistent Healing Prayer

Testimonies inspire faith and remind us that God is still in the healing business. Many people have experienced healing after days, weeks, or even months of persistent prayer.

- A woman with fibromyalgia prayed for months, declaring healing scriptures daily. Over time, all symptoms disappeared!
- A child with asthma was prayed for regularly by his parents. After several months of persistent prayer, he was completely healed.
- A man with back pain kept receiving prayer week after week. One Sunday morning, after months of prayer, he woke up completely pain-free!

These testimonies remind us: Healing does not always happen instantly, but persistence brings results.

Keep Praying Until Healing Manifests

Healing is a promise, but sometimes we must fight for it in prayer. We cannot let delays discourage us. Persistence in prayer is not begging—it is standing in faith until the answer comes.

If you have been praying for healing and have not yet seen results:

- Do not stop believing.
- Keep declaring God's promises.
- Stay surrounded by faith-filled believers.
- Trust that healing is already yours.

Jesus promised,

"Ask, and it will be given to you; seek, and you will find; knock, and it will be opened to you." (Matthew 7:7)

Healing belongs to you—keep knocking until the door opens!

CHAPTER 13

HEALING AS A SIGN OF THE KINGDOM

HEALING IS NOT JUST ABOUT PHYSICAL RESTORATION; it is a sign of the Kingdom of God breaking into the world. Every time Jesus healed the sick, He was demonstrating the presence and power of God's reign. Healing is not an optional extra in the Christian life—it is a manifestation of the Kingdom and a key part of the Gospel.

Throughout the New Testament, we see that wherever the Kingdom of God was preached, healing followed. This is because sickness is a result of the fallen world, and when God's rule is established, sickness must bow to His authority.

This chapter will explore how healing is a sign of God's Kingdom, how Jesus used healing to confirm the Gospel, and how we, as His followers, are called to demonstrate the power of the Kingdom through healing today.

Healing and the Message of the Kingdom

When Jesus came to earth, His central message was:

"Repent, for the Kingdom of Heaven is at hand." (Matthew 4:17)

The Kingdom of God is the realm where God's will is perfectly done—where there is no sickness, no pain, and no oppression. In Revelation 21:4, we see the fullness of the Kingdom:

"He will wipe away every tear from their eyes, and there will be no more death or sorrow or crying or pain. All these things are gone forever."

When Jesus healed the sick, He was giving people a taste of the future Kingdom, showing them what life under God's rule looks like. Healing was not just an act of compassion—it was a sign that God's power had come near.

Jesus Used Healing to Demonstrate the Kingdom

Healing was a major part of Jesus' ministry. Every time He healed, He was proving that the Kingdom of God was breaking into the present world.

- Luke 11:20 – "If I drive out demons by the finger of God, then the Kingdom of God has come upon you."
- Luke 10:9 – "Heal the sick who are there and tell them, 'The Kingdom of God has come near to you.'"

Healing was a confirmation that God's power was present. Wherever the Kingdom advanced, sickness and oppression had to leave.

The Apostles Continued the Kingdom Healing Ministry

After Jesus ascended to heaven, His disciples continued His

healing ministry, proving that healing was not just for His time—
it was part of the ongoing work of the Kingdom.

- Acts 3:6-8 – Peter and John healed a lame man at the
  temple, and many turned to Christ.
- Acts 5:16 – "Crowds gathered also from the towns
  around Jerusalem, bringing their sick and those
  tormented by impure spirits, and all of them were
  healed."
- Acts 8:6-7 – Philip preached the Gospel, and as a
  result, the sick were healed, and demons were cast out.

Healing validated the message of the Gospel. It was a sign that
God's power was real and that Jesus was truly the Messiah.

Healing and Evangelism: A Powerful Combination

Throughout history, healing and miracles have opened doors
for the Gospel. Many revivals and great moves of God have been
accompanied by healing. When people see God's power in action,
their hearts are opened to receive the truth.

- John 4:48 – "Unless you see signs and wonders, you
  will not believe."
- 1 Corinthians 2:4-5 – "My message and my preaching
  were not with persuasive words of wisdom, but with a
  demonstration of the Spirit's power, so that your faith
  might not rest on human wisdom but on God's
  power."

Healing is one of the greatest tools for evangelism. When
people encounter the supernatural power of God, they cannot
deny that He is real.

The Church's Responsibility to Demonstrate the Kingdom

Healing was not meant to stop with the apostles—it was meant to continue through the Church until Jesus returns. Mark 16:17-18 makes it clear that healing is a sign for all believers:

"These signs will accompany those who believe... They will lay hands on the sick, and they will recover."

Every believer is called to be a carrier of the Kingdom, bringing healing and restoration to a broken world.

Healing as a Mandate for Every Christian

Jesus did not say that healing was just for a select few. He told His followers:

"As you go, preach this message: 'The Kingdom of Heaven is near.' Heal the sick, raise the dead, cleanse the lepers, cast out demons. Freely you have received; freely give." (Matthew 10:7-8)

Healing is not optional—it is part of our Kingdom mandate.

Healing Should Be Normal in the Church

James 5:14-15 tells us that healing should be a regular part of church life:

"Is anyone among you sick? Let them call the elders of the church to pray over them and anoint them with oil in the name of the Lord. And the prayer offered in faith will make the sick person well."

The Church should not just talk about healing—it should be actively demonstrating it.

How to Release Healing as a Sign of the Kingdom

If healing is a sign of the Kingdom, how do we step into it? Here are practical steps to release healing:

A. Expect Healing to Happen

Faith is the key to healing. Jesus said:

"According to your faith let it be done to you." (Matthew 9:29)

When we expect miracles, we will see them happen.

B. Boldly Pray for the Sick

Healing happens when we step out in faith. Jesus told us to lay hands on the sick and expect them to recover (Mark 16:18).

The more we pray for healing, the more we will see God's power manifest.

C. Declare the Kingdom Over Sickness

Instead of begging God to heal, declare His Kingdom authority over sickness:

- "In Jesus' name, I command this sickness to leave!"
- "Body, be healed now in the name of Jesus!"
- "The Kingdom of God has come near—be made whole!"

We are ambassadors of the Kingdom, and we have the authority to command sickness to leave.

D. Share Healing Testimonies

Revelation 12:11 says:

"They overcame him by the blood of the Lamb and by the word of their testimony."

Testimonies build faith and invite God to do it again. Every healing is a confirmation that the Kingdom of God is active and advancing.

Healing as a Foretaste of the Future Kingdom

While healing is available now, we know that full healing and restoration will come when Jesus returns. Every miracle we see today is a preview of what is to come.

- Revelation 21:4 – "He will wipe every tear from their eyes. There will be no more death or mourning or crying or pain."
- Romans 8:22-23 – "The whole creation has been groaning as in the pains of childbirth right up to the present time... we wait eagerly for our adoption to sonship, the redemption of our bodies."

Until then, we are called to bring heaven to earth by healing the sick and demonstrating God's power.

Healing Is a Kingdom Assignment

Healing is not just about making people feel better—it is a sign that the Kingdom of God is advancing. Every time someone is healed, we are proclaiming that Jesus is Lord and His reign is breaking into the world.

- Healing confirms the Gospel message.

- Healing reveals the compassion of God.
- Healing is part of the mandate of the Church.
- Healing is a foretaste of the coming Kingdom.

As believers, we are called to heal the sick, demonstrate God's power, and bring the reality of His Kingdom to a broken world. The question is: Will you step out and be part of it?

CHAPTER 14

THE ANOINTING FOR HEALING

HEALING DOES NOT HAPPEN BY HUMAN STRENGTH OR ability—it happens through the power of the Holy Spirit. Throughout Scripture, we see that healing is directly connected to the anointing of God. The anointing is the supernatural empowerment of the Holy Spirit that enables believers to do what they could never do in their own strength. Jesus Himself operated under the anointing when He healed the sick. Acts 10:38 says:

"God anointed Jesus of Nazareth with the Holy Spirit and power, and He went around doing good and healing all who were oppressed by the devil, for God was with Him."

If Jesus needed the anointing to heal, how much more do we? Healing is not about talent, skill, or even religious knowledge—it is about being filled with and empowered by the Holy Spirit.

In this chapter, we will explore the nature of the healing anointing, how to receive it, and how to operate in it effectively.

What Is the Healing Anointing?

The anointing is the manifest presence and power of God that enables believers to bring healing, freedom, and restoration. It is the same power that flowed through Jesus when He touched the sick and cast out demons.

- Isaiah 61:1 – "The Spirit of the Lord God is upon Me, because the Lord has anointed Me to preach good tidings to the poor; He has sent Me to heal the brokenhearted, to proclaim liberty to the captives, and the opening of the prison to those who are bound."
- Luke 4:18 – Jesus read this passage and said, "Today this Scripture is fulfilled in your hearing."

This shows that the healing anointing is part of our Kingdom assignment. It is a heavenly empowerment that allows us to bring healing to a broken world.

How to Receive the Healing Anointing

Many believers desire to operate in healing power, but they do not understand how to receive the anointing. While every Christian has the Holy Spirit living within them, the anointing for healing is something that must be cultivated and activated.

Here are the key steps to receiving and increasing the healing anointing:

A. Pursue Intimacy with God

The anointing flows from relationship, not performance. Jesus spent time in the presence of the Father, and His anointing flowed from that connection.

- John 15:5 – "I am the vine, you are the branches. If you remain in Me and I in you, you will bear much fruit; apart from Me you can do nothing."
- Acts 4:13 – The religious leaders recognized that the disciples had been with Jesus, and that is why they carried His power.

If we want to walk in the anointing, we must spend time in God's presence daily—praying, worshiping, and soaking in His presence.

B. Be Filled with the Holy Spirit

The anointing flows through the baptism of the Holy Spirit. Jesus told His disciples:

"You will receive power when the Holy Spirit comes upon you, and you will be My witnesses." (Acts 1:8)

The baptism of the Holy Spirit is not just about speaking in tongues—it is about receiving supernatural power to do the works of Jesus. If you want to walk in healing power, you must be continually filled with the Holy Spirit (Ephesians 5:18).

C. Walk in Holiness and Obedience

Sin and compromise weaken the anointing. The Holy Spirit flows through clean vessels. While none of us are perfect, we must walk in repentance, obedience, and purity.

- 2 Timothy 2:21 – *"Therefore if anyone cleanses himself from the latter, he will be a vessel for honor, sanctified and useful for the Master, prepared for every good work."*

- Psalm 24:3-4 – *"Who may ascend the hill of the Lord? He who has clean hands and a pure heart."*

The anointing increases in those who live in obedience to God's voice.

D. Develop a Lifestyle of Prayer and Fasting

Prayer and fasting increase the power of the anointing. Jesus said:

"This kind does not go out except by prayer and fasting." (Matthew 17:21)

Fasting:

- Increases sensitivity to the Holy Spirit.
- Breaks demonic strongholds that resist healing.
- Positions you to carry a greater level of power.

Those who desire a strong healing anointing should regularly set aside times for prayer and fasting.

E. Impartation and Laying on of Hands

The healing anointing can also be received through impartation. Throughout the Bible, God transferred His anointing from one person to another through the laying on of hands.

- Numbers 27:18-20 – Moses laid hands on Joshua, imparting spiritual authority.
- 2 Kings 2:9-10 – Elisha received Elijah's double portion anointing.
- Acts 8:17 – The apostles laid hands on believers to receive the Holy Spirit.

If you want to grow in the healing anointing, seek impartation from those who already operate in it. Find mentors, attend healing services, and allow seasoned ministers to pray over you for an increase in the anointing.

How to Release the Healing Anointing

Receiving the anointing is just the beginning—we must also learn how to release it effectively.

A. Lay Hands on the Sick

Mark 16:18 says:

> *"They will lay hands on the sick, and they will recover."*

The healing anointing is transferred through touch. When you lay hands on someone, expect the power of God to flow through you.

B. Speak Healing with Authority

Jesus did not beg for healing—He commanded it. He spoke to sickness as if it was a living thing.

- Mark 9:25 – "You deaf and mute spirit, I command you, come out and never enter again!"
- Luke 8:54 – "Little girl, I say to you, get up!"

When praying for healing, speak directly to the condition and command it to leave in Jesus' name.

C. Recognize When the Anointing Is Flowing

The healing anointing can often be felt. Some signs that the anointing is present include:

- Heat or tingling in your hands.
- A strong sense of faith and boldness.
- The person feeling warmth, electricity, or relief.

When you sense the anointing, press into it—pray boldly and expect healing to manifest.

D. Follow the Holy Spirit's Leading

The Holy Spirit may lead you to:

- Use different methods (e.g., anointing with oil, speaking a word, rebuking a demon).
- Wait in silence and let God move.
- Have the person do something in faith (e.g., move their body, walk, bend over).

Be sensitive to how God wants to move in each situation.

Walking in the Healing Anointing

The healing anointing is available to every believer who is willing to seek God's presence, walk in obedience, and step out in faith. It is not reserved for a special few—it is part of the inheritance of the Church. If you desire to grow in healing ministry, remember:

- Seek God above all else—the anointing flows from relationship.
- Be filled with the Holy Spirit daily.
- Walk in purity, obedience, and faith.

- Practice prayer, fasting, and laying on of hands.
- Step out boldly and expect miracles.

The world is waiting for the manifestation of God's healing power. Will you be one of those who carry and release His anointing?

CHAPTER 15

HEALING, AUTHORITY, AND SPIRITUAL WARFARE

HEALING IS NOT JUST ABOUT PRAYING AND HOPING something happens—it is about exercising authority over sickness and enforcing the victory of Christ. Many times, sickness is not just a natural issue; it is part of a spiritual battle. The enemy seeks to steal, kill, and destroy (John 10:10), and one of the ways he attacks people is through sickness, oppression, and infirmity.

Jesus not only healed the sick—He cast out demons and took authority over sickness. As His disciples, we are called to do the same. Healing is part of spiritual warfare, and to see breakthrough, we must understand how to fight in the Spirit.

In this chapter, we will explore the connection between healing, spiritual warfare, and exercising authority to enforce God's will on earth.

Healing and Spiritual Warfare in the Ministry of Jesus

Jesus did not see sickness as just a physical problem—He often dealt with it as a spiritual attack. Many of His healings involved casting out demons or rebuking sickness as if it were an enemy.

- Luke 13:11-13 – Jesus healed a woman who had been crippled by a spirit of infirmity for 18 years. He did not just pray for her—He declared, "Woman, you are loosed from your infirmity!"
- Matthew 8:16-17 – "When evening had come, they brought to Him many who were demon-possessed. And He cast out the spirits with a word and healed all who were sick."
- Mark 9:25 – Jesus rebuked a deaf and mute spirit, commanding it to leave a boy, and the child was healed.

Jesus understood that some sicknesses are demonic in nature, and He dealt with them by exercising authority.

Understanding Authority in Healing

Jesus did not pray begging prayers—He spoke with authority. He knew that He had been given power over sickness and demons, and He acted on it.

A. The Source of Authority: Jesus' Victory

Before His resurrection, Jesus operated in authority given to Him by the Father. But after His resurrection, He declared:

"All authority has been given to Me in heaven and on earth. Go..."
(Matthew 28:18-19)

Jesus defeated Satan, sickness, and death through His victory on the cross. Because of this, believers now operate from a place of victory, not struggle.

B. Authority Has Been Given to Every Believer

Many Christians pray for healing as if they have no authority, but Jesus clearly gave His authority to His followers.

- Luke 10:19 – "Behold, I give you the authority to trample on serpents and scorpions, and over all the power of the enemy, and nothing shall by any means hurt you."
- Mark 16:17-18 – "These signs will follow those who believe: In My name, they will cast out demons... they will lay hands on the sick, and they will recover."

Authority is not about earning power—it is about knowing who you are in Christ and enforcing His victory.

The Role of Commanding Prayer in Healing

When Jesus and the apostles healed people, they did not ask God to heal—they commanded healing.

A. Jesus Commanded Sickness to Leave

- Mark 1:41-42 – Jesus touched the leper and said, "Be cleansed." Immediately, the leprosy left him.
- Mark 5:41 – To Jairus' daughter, He said, "Little girl, arise!" And she was raised from the dead.
- Luke 7:14 – He touched the coffin of a dead man and said, "Young man, I say to you, arise." And the dead man sat up and began to speak.

B. The Apostles Used the Same Authority

- Acts 3:6-7 – Peter healed the lame man by saying, "In

the name of Jesus Christ of Nazareth, rise up and walk."

- Acts 9:34 – Peter told Aeneas, "Jesus the Christ heals you. Arise and make your bed."

How to Pray with Authority for Healing:

1. Speak directly to the sickness – "In Jesus' name, I command this pain to leave."
2. Declare the person's healing – "Be healed in the name of Jesus."
3. Command the body to align with God's Word – "Nerves, be restored. Muscles, be strengthened."
4. Rebuke any spirit of infirmity – "Spirit of pain, I break your power in Jesus' name."

Recognizing When Sickness Is a Spiritual Attack

Not all sickness is demonic, but some illnesses are caused by spiritual oppression. Here are some signs that a sickness may have a spiritual root:

- Sudden or unexplained illness – A person becomes sick unexpectedly with no medical cause.
- Recurring or generational sickness – A disease runs in the family or keeps coming back.
- Sickness that worsens with prayer – The person gets worse when prayer begins, indicating resistance.
- Sickness accompanied by fear, depression, or nightmares – There may be a spiritual influence causing oppression.

When a sickness is spiritual, it must be addressed through deliverance and prayer warfare.

A. Breaking a Spirit of Infirmity

When sickness has a spiritual root, it is not enough to just pray for healing—the spiritual attack must be broken.

1. Identify the spirit's presence – Ask the Holy Spirit if a spirit of infirmity is involved.
2. Command the spirit to leave – "Spirit of infirmity, I command you to go in Jesus' name."
3. Close the door – If the person has unconfessed sin, bitterness, or fear, lead them to repent and renounce any agreements with the enemy.
4. Speak healing over their body – Declare full restoration.

Engaging in Spiritual Warfare for Healing

Healing prayer is often part of a larger spiritual battle. The enemy does not give up easily, and we must stand firm in faith.

A. Declare God's Promises

Speaking God's Word destroys the lies of the enemy and reinforces what is true. Some powerful healing scriptures include:

- Isaiah 53:5 – "By His stripes, we are healed."
- Psalm 103:2-3 – "He forgives all your iniquities and heals all your diseases."
- Luke 10:19 – "I give you authority over all the power of the enemy."

B. Use the Power of the Blood of Jesus

The blood of Jesus is a weapon against the enemy. When praying for healing, plead the blood of Jesus over the person.

"I cover this body with the blood of Jesus and declare that no weapon formed against it will prosper."

C. Engage in Persistent Prayer

Sometimes healing requires perseverance. Keep praying, fasting, and standing in faith until the breakthrough comes (Luke 18:1-8).

Walking in Authority Over Sickness

Healing is not just about prayer—it is about enforcing the victory of Jesus. As believers, we are called to exercise our authority over sickness, disease, and demonic oppression.

- Know your authority in Christ – You have power over all the enemy's works.
- Pray with boldness – Speak to sickness and command it to leave.
- Recognize spiritual attacks – Some sicknesses require deliverance.
- Stand in faith – Keep declaring healing until it manifests.

When we walk in the authority Jesus gave us, we will see healing, miracles, and breakthroughs manifest in our lives and in those around us.

CHAPTER 16

MINISTERING HEALING IN DIFFERENT SETTINGS

HEALING IS NOT CONFINED TO A CHURCH SERVICE—IT can happen anywhere. Jesus healed people in homes, in the streets, in synagogues, and even at gravesites. The apostles carried healing power into markets, villages, and prisons. Healing is not just for ministers or healing services; it is for every believer in everyday life.

Many Christians assume that healing prayer is only for special occasions or anointed ministers, but the Bible shows us that healing should be a normal part of our daily walk. Whether in a church, a workplace, a hospital, or even a grocery store, believers can release healing wherever they go.

This chapter will explore how to minister healing effectively in different settings, whether in church, at home, in public, or in hospitals.

Healing in Church Gatherings

Church is one of the most natural places to minister healing. The New Testament Church regularly saw miracles, signs, and wonders happening in their gatherings.

- Acts 5:16 – "a multitude gathered from the surrounding cities to Jerusalem, bringing sick people and those who were tormented by unclean spirits, and they were all healed."
- James 5:14-15 – "Is anyone among you sick? Let them call the elders of the church to pray over them and anoint them with oil in the name of the Lord. And the prayer of faith will make the sick person well."

How to Minister Healing in a Church Setting

1. Invite the Presence of the Holy Spirit – Healing happens in God's presence. Before praying, welcome the Holy Spirit into the moment.
2. Use Laying on of Hands and Anointing with Oil – The Bible instructs believers to lay hands on the sick (Mark 16:18) and anoint with oil (James 5:14).
3. Speak Healing with Authority – Do not beg God to heal—command sickness to leave in Jesus' name.
4. Encourage Testimonies – When people are healed, encourage them to share their testimony to build faith.
5. Teach the Congregation to Pray for One Another – Healing is not just for pastors—every believer should pray for the sick.

Healing in Homes and Families

Many of Jesus' miracles happened inside homes. Healing is not just for church services—it should be part of family life.

- Mark 1:30-31 – Jesus healed Peter's mother-in-law in her home.
- Mark 2:1-12 – A paralyzed man was lowered through a roof and healed inside a house.

- Acts 9:33-34 – Peter healed Aeneas, a paralyzed man, in his home.

Praying for Healing at Home

- Teach Your Family About Healing – Parents should teach their children that Jesus still heals today.
- Pray for Family Members When They Are Sick – Instead of just giving medicine, also lay hands on them and pray.
- Break Generational Sickness – If sickness runs in the family, pray to break generational curses (Galatians 3:13).
- Turn Your Home into a Place of Healing – Invite God's presence through worship and prayer so that healing flows naturally.

Many families see healing miracles simply because they expect God to move in their home.

Healing in the Workplace

Healing is a powerful testimony in the workplace. Many people are open to prayer when they are in pain or struggling with sickness.

How to Pray for Healing at Work

- Be Bold but Respectful – If a coworker is sick, say: "Would you mind if I pray for you? It will only take a few seconds."
- Keep It Short and Simple – Workplace prayers should be quick and direct. Example:
- "In Jesus' name, I command this pain to leave right now."

- Follow Up – Ask them how they are feeling later. Many healings are progressive, so follow-up prayer may be needed.
- Share a Testimony – If you have seen healing before, share your experience to build faith.

Healing in the workplace often opens conversations about faith and leads to evangelism opportunities.

Healing in Public Places (Streets, Stores, Parks, etc.)

Jesus healed wherever He went, and we are called to do the same.

- Mark 5:25-34 – A woman was healed in the middle of a crowd.
- Mark 10:46-52 – Bartimaeus was healed on the roadside.
- Acts 3:1-10 – Peter healed a lame man at the temple gate.

How to Minister Healing in Public

1. Be Observant – Look for people who are limping, using crutches, or visibly in pain.
2. Approach with Kindness – Example: "Hey, I couldn't help but notice you're in pain. Would it be okay if I prayed for you real quick?"
3. Keep It Short and Confident – "In Jesus' name, I command healing right now. Pain, go!"
4. Ask Them to Test It Out – After prayer, ask, "Try moving it. Do you feel a difference?"
5. Give Glory to God – If they are healed, say: "Jesus loves you and just touched your body."

6. Healing in public places brings people to Christ and reveals God's love to strangers.

Healing in Hospitals and Nursing Homes

Hospitals and nursing homes are filled with people in need of healing. Jesus often healed those who were bedridden and near death.

- Mark 5:22-24, 35-43 – Jesus healed Jairus' daughter, who was dying.
- John 5:2-9 – Jesus healed a man at the Pool of Bethesda who had been sick for 38 years.
- Acts 9:36-42 – Peter raised Tabitha (Dorcas) from the dead.

How to Minister Healing in Hospitals

1. Be Sensitive to the Person's Faith – Some people are ready to receive healing, while others may need encouragement first.
2. Pray with Authority but Compassion – Speak with boldness, but also be gentle and encouraging.
3. Anoint with Oil if Allowed – James 5:14 encourages anointing the sick with oil.
4. Speak Life Over the Person – Avoid negative words like "I hope this works". Instead, say, "In Jesus' name, I declare complete healing."
5. Encourage Them to Keep Believing – Many healings are progressive, so encourage them to keep standing in faith.

Healing in hospitals is a powerful testimony to doctors and nurses, and it brings hope to families.

Healing in Evangelistic Settings

Healing often opens the door for salvation. In many evangelistic crusades, healings and miracles are what cause people to believe in Jesus.

- Acts 8:5-8 – Philip preached in Samaria, and many were healed. As a result, "there was great joy in the city."
- Acts 14:8-10 – Paul healed a crippled man, and it led to many people believing.

How to Use Healing in Evangelism

- Pray for the Sick in Public Evangelism – If people see miracles, they will believe in Christ.
- Use Healing to Share the Gospel – "Jesus just healed you because He loves you. Have you ever received Him as Lord?"
- Encourage People to Repent and Follow Christ – Healing is not just about physical health—it is about bringing people to salvation.

Healing is a powerful sign that draws people to Christ.

Making Healing a Daily Practice

Healing is not just for special services—it should happen everywhere we go. Jesus commanded us to heal the sick as part of everyday life (Matthew 10:7-8).

- Pray for people regularly.
- Expect miracles wherever you go.
- Be bold and step out in faith.
- Use healing as a tool for evangelism.

The world is waiting to see God's power. Will you be someone who releases healing in everyday life?

CHAPTER 17

OVERCOMING HINDRANCES TO HEALING

While healing is part of God's promise, many believers struggle to receive it. Some have prayed multiple times without results, while others are confused about why healing sometimes takes time or does not seem to manifest at all. The Bible is clear that God's desire is to heal, but certain hindrances can block the flow of healing power.

Healing is not just about praying once and hoping for results —it is about understanding and removing obstacles that may be interfering with God's power. This chapter will explore the most common hindrances to healing and how to overcome them so that healing can manifest fully.

Unbelief and Doubt

One of the greatest barriers to healing is unbelief. Jesus could perform only a few miracles in His hometown because of the people's unbelief.

Mark 6:5-6 – "Now He could do no mighty work there, except that

He laid His hands on a few sick people and healed them. And He marveled because of their unbelief."

Even though Jesus had the full power of God, unbelief limited what He could do. This shows that faith is required to receive healing.

How to Overcome Unbelief:

- Meditate on healing scriptures daily (Romans 10:17).
- Listen to healing testimonies to build your faith.
- Surround yourself with faith-filled believers who encourage healing, not doubt.
- Repent of any unbelief and declare, "Lord, I believe; help my unbelief!" (Mark 9:24).

Faith is the key that activates healing, and doubt is the enemy that blocks it.

Unforgiveness and Bitterness

Jesus directly linked forgiveness with answered prayer. If we are holding onto unforgiveness, it can block healing from manifesting.

- Mark 11:25 – "And whenever you stand praying, if you have anything against anyone, forgive them, that your Father in heaven may also forgive you your trespasses."
- Matthew 6:14-15 – "If you do not forgive others their sins, your Father will not forgive your sins."

Many people suffer from physical pain or sickness because they are carrying bitterness, anger, or resentment.

How to Overcome Unforgiveness:

1. Ask the Holy Spirit to reveal any bitterness in your heart.
2. Make the decision to forgive, even if you don't feel like it.
3. Pray: "Lord, I release this person and bless them in Jesus' name."
4. If possible, reconcile with the person through love and grace.

Many people experience instant healing when they let go of bitterness.

Unconfessed Sin and Strongholds

Some illnesses are linked to sin, disobedience, or spiritual bondage. While not all sickness is caused by sin, the Bible shows that certain sins can open the door to infirmity.

- Psalm 32:3-5 – "When I kept silent, my bones wasted away through my groaning all day long... Then I acknowledged my sin to You... and You forgave the guilt of my sin."
- James 5:16 – "Confess your sins to one another and pray for one another so that you may be healed."

How to Overcome Unconfessed Sin:

1. Repent sincerely and confess any sins to God.
2. Renounce any sinful habits or strongholds.
3. Declare freedom from all guilt, shame, and condemnation.
4. Walk in obedience and holiness, trusting God's grace.

Healing is often connected to spiritual purity. When we remove sin, healing flows more freely.

A Spirit of Infirmity or Demonic Oppression

Some sicknesses are not just medical issues—they are caused by spiritual oppression. The Bible describes people who were physically sick because of demonic influence.

- Luke 13:11-13 – Jesus healed a woman who had been crippled by a spirit of infirmity for 18 years.
- Matthew 9:32-33 – Jesus cast out a demon, and a mute man was instantly able to speak.
- Mark 9:17-29 – A young boy suffered from seizures because of a demonic spirit.

Signs That a Sickness Might Be Spiritual:

- Chronic illness with no medical explanation.
- Pain that moves around the body unpredictably.
- Sickness that gets worse when prayer or worship begins.
- A family history of the same sickness, indicating a generational curse.

How to Overcome a Spirit of Infirmity:

1. Break all agreements with the enemy and renounce sickness.
2. Command the spirit of infirmity to leave in Jesus' name.
3. Speak healing and restoration over the body.
4. Walk in faith, refusing to accept sickness as "normal."

Many sicknesses disappear when people recognize the spiritual nature of the battle and take authority over it.

Lack of Persistence in Prayer

Healing does not always happen instantly—sometimes, it requires persistent prayer.

- Luke 18:1-8 – Jesus told the parable of the persistent widow to show that "men always ought to pray and not lose heart."
- Mark 8:22-25 – Jesus prayed twice for a blind man before his healing was complete.

How to Overcome the Lack of Persistence:

- Do not give up after one prayer—keep pressing in.
- Continue declaring healing even when symptoms remain.
- Be willing to receive prayer multiple times.
- Fast and pray if needed (Matthew 17:21).

Healing is often a battle of faith, and those who persist see results.

Wrong Mindsets About Healing

Many believers have false beliefs that block healing.

- Lie #1: "God might not want to heal me."
- Lie #2: "Maybe God is teaching me a lesson through sickness."
- Lie #3: "Healing is only for special people."
- Lie #4: "It's too late for me to be healed."

How to Overcome Wrong Mindsets:

- Renew your mind with the truth of God's Word (Romans 12:2).
- Reject every lie that contradicts Scripture.
- Confess God's promises and declare healing over your life.

God is always willing to heal (Matthew 8:2-3), and healing is part of the finished work of Christ.

The Power of Speaking Life Over Your Body

Our words have power to bring healing or prolong sickness.

- Proverbs 18:21 – "Death and life are in the power of the tongue."
- Mark 11:23 – "whoever says to this mountain, 'Be removed and be cast into the sea,' and does not doubt in his heart... he will have whatever he says."

How to Speak Life Over Your Body:

- Stop saying, "I'll always be sick" or "I guess I have to live with this."
- Start saying, "I am healed in Jesus' name" and "Sickness has no place in my body."
- Declare Scripture daily over your body.

Many believers stay sick because they speak words of sickness instead of speaking words of life.

Removing Every Barrier to Healing

If healing has been delayed, ask the Holy Spirit to reveal any hindrances. Healing is God's will, and He wants you to receive it fully.

- Build your faith and remove doubt.
- Forgive others and release bitterness.
- Confess and renounce any sin or generational curses.
- Take authority over demonic sickness.
- Persist in prayer until healing manifests.
- Speak life over your body daily.

Healing belongs to you—remove every obstacle and walk in the fullness of what Jesus paid for!

CHAPTER 18

MAINTAINING HEALING AND WALKING IN DIVINE HEALTH

RECEIVING HEALING IS POWERFUL, BUT MAINTAINING healing and walking in divine health is just as important. Many believers experience healing, only to find that symptoms return after some time. Others are healed but do not know how to stay in a place of faith and protection from future sickness.

Healing is not just about one-time miracles—it is about living in divine health as part of our covenant with God. Walking in divine health means living in a way that prevents sickness, disease, and spiritual attacks from taking hold in our lives.

In this chapter, we will explore how to maintain healing, how to prevent sickness from returning, and how to live in the fullness of God's health and wholeness every day.

Healing Must Be Guarded

Healing is not automatic—it must be protected. Jesus warned people to be vigilant after receiving healing.

- John 5:14 – Jesus told the healed man, "See, you have been made well. Sin no more, lest a worse thing come upon you."
- Matthew 12:43-45 – Jesus explained that when an unclean spirit leaves a person, it may try to return with greater force.

This means that after healing, the enemy may try to bring back symptoms, doubts, or fear to make you believe that your healing was not real. How to Guard Your Healing:

- Refuse to accept returning symptoms. Speak against them and declare, "I have been healed, and I reject this sickness in Jesus' name!"
- Continue declaring healing scriptures daily.
- Stay in faith and do not allow doubt to take root.
- Surround yourself with people who encourage healing, not fear.

Healing is not just about receiving—it is about stewarding what God has given you.

Speaking Life Over Your Body

Our words have power. The Bible teaches that what we speak over ourselves affects our health and well-being.

- Proverbs 18:21 – "Death and life are in the power of the tongue."
- Mark 11:23 – "For assuredly, I say to you, whoever says to this mountain, 'Be removed and be cast into the sea,' and does not doubt in his heart, but believes that those things he says will be done, he will have whatever he says."

Avoid Saying:

- •"I guess the sickness is back."
- •"I always get sick this time of year."
- •"I hope this healing lasts."

Instead, Declare:

- "I walk in divine health daily."
- "Sickness has no place in my body."
- "The same Spirit that raised Jesus from the dead gives life to my body" (Romans 8:11).

Healing is reinforced through what you speak.

Daily Communion: A Weapon for Divine Health

The Lord's Supper is not just a ritual—it is a supernatural act that sustains health and healing. The early church practiced it daily (Acts 2:46), and it was considered a source of divine life. Paul taught that many people were sick and dying early because they did not discern the power of communion.

1 Corinthians 11:29-30 – "For he who eats and drinks in an unworthy manner eats and drinks judgment to himself, not discerning the Lord's body. That is why many among you are weak and sick, and some have died."

Communion reminds us that Jesus carried our sicknesses and that His body was broken for our healing (Isaiah 53:5). How to Use Communion for Divine Health:

1. Take it regularly—not just at church, but also in your personal time with God.

2. Declare healing as you partake—say, "By His stripes, I am healed!"
3. Use it as a weapon against sickness—if symptoms arise, take communion and remind your body of Christ's finished work.

Many believers testify that regular communion strengthens their bodies and keeps sickness away.

Staying in God's Presence

Healing flows from God's presence. The more we dwell in His presence, the more we walk in divine health.

Psalm 91:1, 10 – "He who dwells in the secret place of the Most High shall abide under the shadow of the Almighty... No evil shall befall you, Nor shall any plague come near your dwelling;"

Healing is not just about receiving a touch from God—it is about abiding in Him daily.

Ways to Stay in God's Presence for Health:

- Daily prayer and worship—healing is found in God's presence.
- Meditate on the Word—healing flows from God's truth.
- Fasting and seeking God—breakthrough often comes through spiritual discipline.

People who cultivate a strong connection with God often walk in long-term health and strength.

Living a Healthy Lifestyle

While healing is supernatural, we are also called to steward our bodies wisely. Many believers receive healing but do not take care of their physical health, leading to problems later.

1 Corinthians 6:19-20 – "Do you not know that your body is the temple of the Holy Spirit? Therefore, honor God with your body."

Practical Steps for Divine Health:

- Eat nutritious foods that strengthen the body.
- Get proper rest—the body needs time to recover and recharge.
- Exercise and stay active—physical movement keeps the body strong.
- Avoid stress—stress weakens the immune system and invites sickness.

God's supernatural healing does not replace taking care of our bodies—it works alongside wisdom and stewardship.

Resisting the Enemy's Attacks

The devil will try to steal your healing by attacking with fear, doubt, and lying symptoms.

- John 10:10 – *"The thief does not come except to steal, and to kill, and to destroy. I have come that they may have life, and that they may have it more abundantly."*
- 1 Peter 5:8-9 – *"Be sober, be vigilant; because your adversary the devil walks about like a roaring lion, seeking whom he may devour. Resist him, steadfast in the faith"*

How to Resist the Enemy's Attacks:

1. Rebuke symptoms immediately—Do not tolerate sickness; speak against it.
2. Use the Word of God—Declare healing scriptures over your body.
3. Keep your mind renewed—Do not let fear or doubt take root.
4. Surround yourself with faith-filled believers—Avoid negative influences.

Healing is not just a one-time event—it is a daily battle to stand in victory.

Walking in a Lifestyle of Healing

Many believers experience healing only once in a while, but God's desire is that we live in a continuous flow of health and wholeness. Divine health means that:

- Sickness is rare in your life.
- You recover quickly when attacks come.
- You experience supernatural strength and vitality.
- You carry healing to others wherever you go.

Keys to Walking in Divine Health Daily:

- Live a lifestyle of faith and prayer.
- Take communion regularly.
- Declare healing scriptures over yourself.
- Stay in an atmosphere of worship and God's presence.
- Walk in obedience to God's Word.

Divine health is God's will, and it is available to every believer who chooses to walk in it daily.

Living in the Fullness of God's Healing Power

Healing is not meant to be a one-time event—it is a way of life. By maintaining faith, resisting the enemy, and staying in God's presence, we can experience ongoing health and strength.

- Guard your healing.
- Speak life over your body.
- Use communion as a tool for divine health.
- Stay connected to God's presence.
- Live with wisdom and discipline.

Healing is not just about being healed—it is about living in divine health every day. Will you step into that reality?

CHAPTER 19

ACTIVATING THE HEALING MINISTRY IN YOUR LIFE

HEALING IS NOT JUST FOR A SELECT FEW—IT IS FOR every believer. Jesus made it clear that healing was part of the Great Commission, and every follower of Christ is called to lay hands on the sick and see them recover (Mark 16:17-18). Yet many believers hesitate to pray for the sick because they feel unqualified, fearful, or unsure of what to do.

Healing is not about our ability—it is about God's power working through us. This final chapter will equip you to step into healing ministry with boldness, showing you how to activate God's healing power and see miracles happen in your daily life.

Every Believer Is Called to Heal the Sick

Healing was never meant to be limited to pastors or evangelists. Jesus commanded all His disciples to heal the sick, raise the dead, and cast out demons (Matthew 10:7-8).

- Mark 16:17-18 – "These signs will follow those who believe: In My name, they will cast out demons... they will lay hands on the sick, and they will recover."

- John 14:12 – "Whoever believes in Me will do the works that I have been doing, and they will do even greater things."

If you are a believer, healing is part of your calling. You do not need a title or special training—you simply need faith and obedience.

Overcoming Fear and Hesitation

Many Christians hesitate to pray for healing because of fear:

- Fear of failure – "What if nothing happens?"
- Fear of rejection – "What if they don't want prayer?"
- Fear of looking foolish – "What if people think I'm crazy?"

How to Overcome These Fears:

1. Remember, healing is God's responsibility, not yours – Your job is to pray; God's job is to heal.
2. Step out in obedience – Miracles happen when we take action, not when we wait for perfect conditions.
3. Remind yourself of God's promises – Speak verses like "The same Spirit that raised Jesus from the dead lives in me" (Romans 8:11).
4. Start small – Pray for friends and family before stepping out in public.

Faith grows as we use it. The more you pray for healing, the more you will see results.

The Healing Model: A Simple Five-Step Process

Many people overcomplicate healing ministry. But Jesus

modeled a simple approach that we can follow. Here is a five-step model that will help you confidently pray for the sick.

Step 1: Ask Questions and Listen

Before praying, find out:

- What is wrong? (Physical pain? Sickness? Emotional wound?)
- How long have they had it?
- Has anything helped or made it worse?
- Do they believe Jesus can heal them?

Listening allows you to pray with wisdom and compassion.

Step 2: Invite the Presence of the Holy Spirit

Before laying hands on the sick, take a moment to invite the Holy Spirit to come and move. Healing is not just about words—it is about God's power manifesting. Example:

"Holy Spirit, I welcome You here. I invite Your healing presence right now."

Step 3: Pray with Authority

Instead of begging God to heal, speak directly to the condition with boldness.

- "In the name of Jesus, I command this pain to leave."
- "I declare healing in this body right now."
- "Every sickness, be gone in Jesus' name."

Jesus never prayed long prayers for healing—He spoke with authority and expected results.

Step 4: Ask the Person to Check for Change

After praying, ask:

- "Do you feel any different?"
- "Has the pain decreased?"
- "Try to move—do you notice a change?"

If they experience partial healing, pray again. Jesus prayed twice for the blind man in Mark 8:22-25. Persistence leads to greater breakthroughs.

Step 5: Encourage and Follow Up

Whether healing is immediate or progressive, encourage them to:

- Thank God for their healing.
- Keep declaring God's promises.
- Continue believing even if symptoms try to return.

If full healing does not happen immediately, reassure them:

"God is working, and we will keep standing in faith together!"

Where to Minister Healing

Healing is not just for church services—it should happen everywhere.

A. Healing at Church

- Pray for people at the altar or in small groups.
- Encourage church members to pray for each other.
- Share healing testimonies to build faith.

B. Healing at Home

- Pray for family members regularly.
- Lay hands on children when they are sick.
- Break generational curses and sicknesses.

C. Healing in Public

- Offer to pray for coworkers.
- Ask strangers if they need prayer (many are open!).
- Watch for people with crutches, casts, or pain, and approach them with love.

D. Healing in Hospitals or Nursing Homes

- Pray for the sick in hospitals.
- Release God's presence in medical settings.
- Comfort and encourage families believing for healing.

Healing happens wherever we step out in faith.

Ministering Healing with Love and Compassion

Healing is not just about power—it is about love. Jesus was moved by compassion when He healed the sick.

- Matthew 14:14 – *"And when Jesus went out He saw a great multitude; and He was moved with compassion for them, and healed their sick.."*
- Luke 7:13-15 – Jesus was moved by compassion and raised a widow's son from the dead.

How to Minister Healing with Compassion:

- Listen to people's pain and struggles.

- Treat them with kindness and dignity.
- Pray in a way that brings comfort, not fear.
- Point them to Jesus, not just to the healing.

People need to know that healing is not just about fixing problems—it is about encountering God's love.

Expect Miracles and Keep Growing

Healing ministry is a journey, and the more you step out, the more you will see God's power in action.

A. Expect Miracles

- Go into every prayer expecting God to move.
- Celebrate every healing, no matter how small.
- Keep praying and believing, even when results are delayed.

B. Keep Growing in Healing Ministry

- Study healing scriptures and renew your faith.
- Listen to testimonies to build expectation.
- Attend healing conferences or get training.
- Find a mentor who operates in healing.

Faith for healing grows as we exercise it.

Your Role in the Healing Movement

Healing is not just about receiving miracles—it is about becoming someone who releases healing to others. Jesus is raising up a generation of believers who will walk in divine health, minister healing, and bring the power of the Kingdom to the world.

- Healing is for every believer.
- Fear must be overcome with boldness.
- Healing happens when we step out in faith.
- Everywhere we go, God wants to heal.
- Compassion is the key to releasing miracles.

This book has given you the tools and biblical foundations to step into healing ministry. Now, the question is:

Will you say yes to God's call to heal the sick? The world is waiting. The sick are waiting. The broken are waiting. It's time to step out and release God's healing power wherever you go.

Final Prayer of Activation:

"Father, I thank You that healing is part of the Kingdom and that You have called me to walk in Your power. I receive the authority Jesus has given me to heal the sick. I ask You to fill me with boldness and compassion so that I may release Your healing power everywhere I go. Use my hands, my words, and my prayers to bring healing to those in need. I commit to stepping out in faith and believing that You will move. I am a vessel of Your healing power, and I will see miracles in Jesus' name. Amen!"

CONCLUSION

THE COMMISSION YOU
CAN NO LONGER IGNORE

There comes a moment in every believer's life when the truth of God's Word refuses to remain merely inspiring—it becomes unavoidable. It stops being something you admire and becomes something you are accountable for. It stops being theology you agree with and becomes a mantle you must wear. It stops being a possibility and becomes a mandate.

This is that moment.

Everything you have read in this book has been leading you here: to a line in the sand, to a divine confrontation, to a holy invitation that can no longer be postponed, delegated, or excused.

You have now seen—clearly, undeniably, repeatedly—that healing is not a side ministry, an optional emphasis, or a charismatic curiosity. Healing is the public announcement that the Kingdom of God has invaded the kingdom of darkness. It is the visible proof that Jesus is alive and reigning. It is the inheritance of every believer and the responsibility of every disciple.

Nothing in the life of Jesus, the Gospels, the book of Acts, or the teaching of the apostles gives you permission to be passive about healing. Nothing in Scripture allows you to believe that healing is only for the gifted few. Nothing in God's nature suggests that the sick are meant to remain in bondage so long as believers remain silent.

You cannot unread what you now know.
You cannot unknow what the Word has revealed.
You cannot retreat to a version of Christianity that excuses powerlessness.
Healing is part of the Gospel.
Healing is part of the Kingdom.
Healing is part of your calling.

And that means one thing: **you are now responsible for what you carry.**

The Moment God Holds You Accountable For

The entire book has been one long unveiling—not only of healing, but of *your role* in it.

You've seen...

- **Faith** is not a suggestion; it is the environment where healing lives.
- **Persistence** is not a last resort; it is a Kingdom strategy.
- **Authority** is not a metaphor; it is a weapon.
- **The anointing** is not emotional energy; it is the power of the Holy Spirit made manifest.
- **Removing hindrances** is not optional; it is part of the battle.

- **Divine health** is not reserved for the elite; it is your covenant.
- **Activation** is not for the pulpit; it is for every believer in every place at every moment.

If you finish this book and do nothing differently, then you have only educated yourself—you have not obeyed Jesus. But this book was never meant to entertain your mind. It was meant to provoke your spirit.

What you have read is not schooling.
It is a *summons*.

The King Has Already Spoken—Now You Must Answer

Jesus never separated the message of the Kingdom from the demonstration of the Kingdom. He did not preach healing as an idea—He manifested healing as reality. And He never once said, "Admire what I do." He said, **"Follow Me."**

To follow Him is to do what He did.
To believe in Him is to continue His works.
To be filled with His Spirit is to carry His ministry.

The healing ministry is not a specialty.

It is sonship expressed.
It is discipleship lived.
It is the Kingdom enforced.
It is the Gospel confirmed.

Jesus healed the sick because the Kingdom had come near. The apostles healed the sick because the Kingdom had been handed to them. You heal the sick because the Kingdom is now inside you.

There is no Christianity in Scripture that is powerless.
There is no discipleship in the Bible that avoids risk.
There is no following of Jesus that does not confront sickness and darkness.

If your Christianity has made room for the sick to remain sick while the healer inside you remains silent, then something must change. And that change begins with you.

The Enemy Hoped You Would Stay Ignorant—Now He Hopes You Stay Afraid

One of Satan's greatest strategies has been convincing believers that healing is complicated, unpredictable, or reserved for the spiritually elite. He knows that the day the average believer realizes healing is simple, normal, and expected—that is the day he loses millions of people he has held in bondage. You have just spent twenty chapters dismantling the enemy's lies:

- You now know sickness is part of the fall, not the Father's plan.
- You now know healing is a manifestation of the Kingdom, not a rare miracle.
- You now know you carry authority, not weakness.
- You now know faith is a choice, not a feeling.
- You now know persistence is victory, not desperation.
- You now know the anointing is for you, not for "special" ministers.
- You now know hindrances can be removed, not endured.
- You now know divine health is accessible, not theoretical.
- You now know activation is commanded, not optional.

So the only strategy left for the enemy...
...is to hope you stay passive.

He cannot unteach what God has revealed to you.
He cannot undo the Scriptures you've encountered.
He cannot erase the revelation you've received.

He can only whisper fear, intimidation, hesitation, and self-doubt. He hopes you will be too nervous to pray, too insecure to speak, too timid to lay hands, too unsure to act. Hell fears your obedience far more than your knowledge. He is not threatened by what you read. He is threatened by what you do. And this conclusion is God's way of telling you: *Do something.*

You Were Never Meant to Be a Spectator in the Kingdom

Every believer who walks into a hospital, workplace, school, house, or grocery store is a walking collision between two kingdoms. You don't "bring" healing with you—you carry the Healer. You don't carry potential miracles—you carry the Miracle Worker.

The Kingdom is not just something you announce.
The Kingdom is something you release.

You are not waiting for revival.
Revival is waiting for you.

You are not waiting for the right moment.
Every moment is the right moment.

You are not waiting for a healing service.
Your life *is* the healing service.

The apostles didn't wait for pulpits—they created altars in the streets. They didn't wait for permission—they moved with conviction. They didn't wait for the atmosphere to be perfect—they shifted the atmosphere by acting in faith.

There is no such thing as a passive apostolic believer. There is no such thing as a powerless Spirit-filled Christian. There is no such thing as a silent carrier of the healing anointing.

You were born to enforce the victory of Jesus. You were redeemed to destroy the works of the devil. You were commissioned to announce and demonstrate the Kingdom. Nothing about you was made for hiding. Everything about you was made for healing.

The Kingdom Needs Your Hands, Not Just Your Amen

You already know the theology.
You already understand the foundations.
You already see the biblical patterns.
You already recognize the authority you carry.

But none of it matters until someone gets healed *through your hands*. Your hands are meant to glow with the life of the Spirit. Your voice is meant to carry the authority of Jesus. Your presence is meant to shift sickness out of people's bodies. Your obedience is meant to bring heaven into ordinary moments.

The world has enough teaching. What it needs is demonstration. It has enough opinions. What it needs is power. It has enough religion. What it needs is Kingdom. And the Kingdom is revealed when people like you stop waiting for the perfect moment and start obeying in the present moment.

What You Carry Now Demands a Response

This book has equipped you with:

- the theology of healing,
- the faith that activates healing,
- the persistence that sustains healing,
- the authority that enforces healing,
- the anointing that releases healing,
- the discernment that protects healing,
- the lifestyle that maintains healing,
- and the boldness that multiplies healing.

You cannot finish this journey and remain unchanged.
You cannot honor the revelation by simply admiring it.
You honor it by *obeying* it.

Healing is now your responsibility. Not because you are gifted, but because you are His. Not because you feel ready, but because the sick cannot wait. Not because you are powerful, but because Jesus is.

You have been entrusted with truth that demands expression. You have been given tools that demand use. You have been filled with a Spirit who demands movement. The God who heals lives inside you—and He is ready to be revealed.

The Question Heaven Is Asking You Right Now

It is not:
"Do you understand healing?"
You do.

It is not:
"Are you called to healing?"
You are.

It is not:
"Do you have authority?"
You have more than enough.

The question heaven is asking is far simpler and far more dangerous:

"Will you obey?"

- Will you pray for the sick when you feel nothing?
- Will you lay hands on strangers when fear whispers in your ear?
- Will you open your mouth when intimidation tells you to stay quiet?
- Will you stand in faith when symptoms persist?
- Will you cast out demons when oppression manifests?
- Will you proclaim the Kingdom when culture pushes back?
- Will you steward the anointing when the cost feels high?
- Will you confront sickness instead of accommodating it?
- Will you become the answer instead of waiting for one?

This is not a gentle invitation. This is a royal commissioning. The King of Glory is not suggesting something to you. He is commanding you:

"Heal the sick."

And you must answer Him.

You Are Being Sent Out—Right Now

The conclusion of this book is not the end of something—it is the beginning. The Spirit of God is stirring you to move:

- into homes where fear has settled,
- into hospitals where hope has drained,
- into workplaces where sickness steals joy,
- into churches where faith needs revival,
- into streets where darkness dominates,
- into families that need breakthrough,
- into lives that are waiting for someone bold enough to act.

Why not you?
Why not now?
Why not today?

The Kingdom of God does not advance through caution—it advances through courage. It does not move through theory—it moves through obedience. It does not spread through the extraordinary few—it spreads through the faithful many.

Jesus is ready to heal through you.
The Spirit is ready to flow through you.
The Father is ready to confirm His Word through you.

The sick are not waiting for better sermons—they are waiting for you. The oppressed are not waiting for more conferences—they are waiting for you. The broken are not waiting for better explanations—they are waiting for you.

You have been thoroughly equipped.
You have been deeply taught.
You have been faithfully prepared.

Now heaven is saying: *"Go."*

A Final Charge Before You Step Out

If you want healing to mark your life, it will require:
Boldness when fear rises.
Obedience when hesitation creeps in.
Faith when symptoms remain.
Persistence when breakthroughs delay.
Authority when spirits resist.
Compassion when people are broken.
Anointing fueled by intimacy.
Discernment sharpened by Scripture.
Purity guarded by holiness.
Humility shaped by surrender.

You will not always feel ready—but God will always be with you. You will not always see immediate results—but power will flow when you obey. You will not always understand every battle —but victory belongs to the name you carry. This world is not waiting for another book on healing It is waiting for believers who live healing.

Be one of them.

A Prophetic Commissioning Over Your Life

Read this slowly. Let it become the cry of your spirit:

"Jesus, I step into my calling.
I embrace the healing ministry You entrusted to every believer.
I refuse passivity, fear, and hesitation.
I choose boldness, faith, and obedience.
My hands are Yours—use them for healing.
My voice is Yours—use it with authority.
My life is Yours—use it for Your Kingdom.
I will heal the sick.

I will cast out demons.
I will release the Kingdom.
I will obey the Great Commission.
I say yes to the call of God.
And I will not turn back."

This is your moment.
Your turning point.
Your commissioning.
Your awakening.
Your yes.

Healing is no longer a topic you studied. It is now a mantle you carry.

Now go...
heal the sick, cast out demons, proclaim the Kingdom, and do it until you see Him face to face.

This is your assignment.
This is your call.
This is your life.

And this is just the beginning.

ABOUT THE AUTHOR

Tom Cornell is the Senior Leader of SOZO Church in Washington state, founder of Walk in the Light International and SOZO Network. Tom is married to his beautiful wife Katy and lives in the Puget Sound area with her and their three kids. He has been in ministry pastoring and teaching the body of Christ since 2008.

He has a passion to see the body of Christ moving from people with an orphan mindset to that of sonship; equipping the body to do the work of Jesus resulting in seeing the Kingdom of God manifested here on earth.

www.ingramcontent.com/pod-product-compliance
Lightning Source LLC
LaVergne TN
LVHW052029080426
835513LV00018B/2237